T0388794

Return to Joy

THE LIFELONG IMPACT OF FATHER-WOUNDING
AND PATHWAYS TO HEALING

Keith Kahle, MD

LITTLE CREEK PRESS

MINERAL POINT, WISCONSIN

Little Creek Press
5341 Sunny Ridge Road
Mineral Point, WI 53565

ORDERING INFORMATION
Quantity sales. Special discounts are available on quantity purchases by corporations, associations, and others. For details, contact info@littlecreekpress.com

Printed in the United States of America

Cataloging-in-Publication Data
Name: Keith Kahle, author
Title: Return to Joy: The Lifelong Impact of Father-Wounding and Pathways to Healing
Description: Mineral Point, WI Little Creek Press, 2025
Identifiers: LCCN: 2025914543 | ISBN: 978-1-967311-80-4
Classification: SELF-HELP / Personal Growth / Self-Esteem
BIOGRAPHY & AUTOBIOGRAPHY / Personal Memoirs
PSYCHOLOGY / Mental Health

Book design by Little Creek Press

Kintsugi is the Japanese art of repairing broken pottery using lacquer mixed with powdered gold, silver, or platinum. Rather than hiding the damage, Kintsugi highlights it—embracing flaws and treating them as part of the object's history. The result is a piece made more beautiful and unique by its imperfections, symbolizing resilience, healing, and the beauty of embracing what is broken.

for my fellow bushwhackers

Contents

Author's Note

I have included several references to my life as an orthopedic surgeon in this book, which is why I decided to add the MD after my name as its author. It would have seemed odd not to do so. However, I am not a mental health or medical expert, and no suggestion I make here, explicit or implied, is intended as a substitute for consultation with licensed practitioners who specialize in these areas. All matters regarding your health require medical supervision. Neither the author nor the publisher shall be liable or responsible for any loss or damage allegedly arising from any information or suggestion in this book.

I also wrote about my personal experiences with MDMA, also known as ecstasy or molly, which is currently an illegal drug that appears on Schedule I of the US Controlled Substances Act. There is a great deal of scientific and public interest in the potential of MDMA to alleviate the debilitating symptoms of post-traumatic stress disorder. Nevertheless, readers are strongly advised to consult with appropriate experts in medicine and criminal law about the risks of using MDMA before making any decision to do so.

Preface

When you hear hoofbeats, don't think of zebras. Every first-year medical student learns this pithy reminder that common things are common and uncommon things are not. That's not to say that uncommon things never happen, but it teaches a young doctor to at least put his money on horses unless he's in Africa.

It takes at least ten thousand hours of practice to become an expert at anything, and repetition to the point of pattern recognition is why a chess grandmaster can walk around a room and win games against twenty good players at the same time, and how quarterback Tom Brady could pick apart any defense in his forties. Over and over, they've seen every pattern, every outcome of decisions they've made, and they know what their opponent will do without having to think about it. Elders, too, have this talent, and the long learning curve of pattern recognition related to human behavior is why elders are usually elderly. The main difference between elders and old cynics is that elders have seen enough grace in their lives to still believe in zebras.

Father-wounding is extremely common, especially among males, and there are predictable patterns of how this form of childhood trauma makes us feel and behave throughout our lives. However, most people are unaware of these patterns for several reasons:

- Whenever you have an emotional reaction, an old wound has been triggered, but most of us have poor recall of the childhood events that created those wounds.
- It's very hard to connect the dots between things your father did or failed to do when you were a child and your loneliness and troubled marriage at fifty.
- Fathers no longer teach their sons about the holy mysteries and normal passages of life, as they did for millennia through male rites of initiation. Serious shit predictably happens in people's lives between about the ages of thirty-five and sixty, but we never see it coming and are shocked when we get sick, marriages fall apart, priests leave the priesthood, and Green Bay Packers future Hall of Fame quarterbacks get traded to the Jets.
- Male individualism is a cultural norm that keeps us in the dark. Most men lead private, competitive lives driven by ambition to stand out from the crowd. This makes it very hard to accept the reality that we all, more or less, think the same way, do the same things, and struggle with the same stuff. The one path we travel through life is wide and well-worn, but men insist upon blazing their own trails, so we line up and take turns stumbling over the same boulders and falling off the same cliffs. The half of our species that

never asks for directions is composed almost entirely of solo bushwhackers. Boys should all be issued little Fisher-Price machetes when they start school.

Even nonviolent father-wounding is still trauma, and we pay a shockingly high price for it: Traumatized people are universally deprived of pleasure and joy, live in the past, don't like themselves, feel ashamed of the traumas they experienced and the choices they made to survive, are physiologically battered by emotional reactivity, and have great difficulty negotiating intimate relationships. Does this sound familiar?

The first step of healing is recognizing that you're wounded rather than defective. This isn't as simple as it sounds, but once you really know this about yourself, you can stop spinning your wheels, quit beating yourself up, and begin to explore trauma-related therapeutic options. Healing is a difficult journey that's made even harder by the fact that almost no one feels comfortable applying the words *trauma* and *shame* to their painful experiences. Yet, understanding these ever-present realities of father-wounding can greatly facilitate healing.

I sometimes think that my hard-won wisdom and many years of experience should have transformed me into a superhero who can leap over tall buildings, fix problems, and head off disasters. However, the true gift of being an elder is a wonderfully enhanced capacity for gratitude and joy that walks hand in hand with heartache. This is not a season of winning; it's a season of showing up, deep friendships, and creating safe spaces for open hearts.

I wrote primarily to men about father-wounding as my point of view because that's what I know from personal experience and because it's so prevalent among males. However, my journey has filled me with compassion for the legions of men *and* women whose parental relationships have led them to believe that they are unworthy of love, kindness, and respect. *Return to Joy* is for all of you.

I didn't write this book to bash anyone's dad, including my own, or to elucidate the seven habits of transformed men. I wrote it because garden-variety father-wounding such as mine is so commonplace as to be considered normal and so seemingly benign that its pernicious nature is hidden in plain sight. I hope my stories will help with pattern recognition in your life and lead to deep conversations with wise people who know and love you.

Introduction

In 1935, Austrian researcher Konrad Lorenz hatched a greylag goose that he named Martina. In an endearing case of mistaken identity, Lorenz was the first moving thing that Martina saw after she emerged from her eggshell, and she imprinted on him as her mother, following him everywhere he went and even sleeping in his bedroom. Lorenz postulated that imprinting—what we now call attachment—occurs during a brief critical period of brain development in newly hatched geese as a survival benefit. He later won a Nobel Prize for his work on this issue.

A well-intentioned parent can easily convince a sensitive child that he or she is an ugly duckling; this was my experience growing up. My father was a good man, and I knew that he loved me, but life was hard for him, and he was chronically irritable and depressed. I don't recall ever hearing these exact words, but his messaging was loud and clear: "Go away. Leave me alone. Don't bother me." Somewhere along the line, I became convinced that there was something wrong with me, something irritating that made me unworthy of his love. I was just a kid; how could it be otherwise? This core message of shame became subconsciously fixed in my mind as a boy, and it hardened into the dingy lens through which I saw myself and interpreted my intimate relationships throughout my life.

A few years ago I was diagnosed with cataracts, which is a clouding of the lenses of the eyes that occurs commonly in old folks. New glasses didn't improve my vision, so I underwent surgery on both eyes, two weeks apart. Cataract surgery involves making a small incision along the edge of the cornea, removing the cloudy lens behind it, and inserting a clear artificial lens. During the two weeks between surgeries, I often compared my vision in the operated eye with that of the unoperated one, and I was shocked by the differences, especially in my perception of whiteness. What I had long perceived as white was, in fact, quite dingy and yellowish, but my cataracts had built up so slowly over a period of years that I had never noticed the dulling. After surgery, I often remarked how beautiful the world really was.

Cataracts also occur at the other end of the age spectrum. Three or four children out of every ten thousand live births are born each year with congenital cataracts, and if corrective eye surgery isn't performed early in life, these children will never be able to see. This is because a critical period of brain development related to vision closes by five years of age. Figuring out how to reopen closed critical periods of brain plasticity to facilitate healing for this and other disabling conditions, including PTSD, is the holy grail of neuroscience. Research has shown that psychedelic drugs have the unique capacity to reopen these critical periods. Still, until safe and effective medications become widely available, teaching old dogs new tricks will continue to be hard. *Woof!*

I have come to understand father-wounding as a form of childhood trauma that creates a "cataract of the soul" during a critical period of brain development. We all come into this world with a clean slate, having never been lied to about our worthiness, but early childhood is a period of great vulnerability to messaging about who we are. Father-wounding is a major producer of mistaken identities, and the tricky thing is that it doesn't make you feel like you're wounded. It makes you feel like you're bad.

What was it like to observe life through my cataract of the soul? Despite being very successful in many ways, I saw myself as a problem: burdensome, never good enough. I was blind to how lovable I truly was, which made me highly reactive to any perceived rejection or criticism. My minefield of sensitivities was the size of a football field, and I had to be handled with care, lest I feel hurt and retreat into my silent tower of self-sufficiency. I never really felt safe. I was exhausted from constantly wearing a ton of armor and frustrated by never having enough Band-Aids. There was no escape from the incessant voice of my inner critic, and I experienced only the absence of God despite an abundance of churching.

Well, I'm an old man now, and my cataract of the soul is finally gone. I see life through the clear lens of my true identity and know how deeply I am loved. I know *who* I am and *whose* I am, I rarely feel shame or fear, and my tank is overflowing. My minefield of sensitivities has shrunk to the size of a pack of

Lucky Strikes. I've been in a season of joy for a long time, and I know it's not just a passing phenomenon. After a half-century odyssey, I've come home to a familiar place and smell cookies baking in the oven. I had no idea that life could be this good, especially given so much evidence to the contrary.

This is my story of garden-variety father-wounding—of small-t trauma with large-C consequences—and of recovery. I hope it will help to light your path, perhaps shorten your journey, and give you confidence that it's never too late to experience healing.

1

Ed

When I was an orthopedic surgeon in the Air Force many years ago, I operated on a ninety-year-old retiree for a fractured hip. Back then, patients stayed in the hospital for a week or so after surgery of this type, and during his postoperative hospitalization, I started getting a lot of complaints from the nursing staff about Ed's behavior. They said he was demanding, unappreciative, and highly critical of their care. In addition, he constantly bragged about his accomplishments and the important people he knew. He was such a difficult patient that the nurses had started drawing straws to see who had to take care of him.

I was on call one evening and had to be at the hospital anyway, so I decided to drop by and get to know Ed a little better. I pulled up a chair next to his bed, and we started chatting about his life. He had been a high-ranking officer during his military career and later became CEO of a well-known company. Ed was happy to share stories of his many accomplishments with me, and I was genuinely impressed.

I had noticed he never had visitors, so I asked about his family and friends. He'd been married twice, was now single, and lived alone. He didn't seem to have any close friends and was estranged from his two sons. I could tell that it was upsetting him to talk about this, so I switched topics and asked where he grew up and what life was like for him as a kid. He shared a couple of humorous anecdotes from his childhood and then became quiet and closed his eyes. After several minutes of silence, I assumed he'd fallen asleep.

As I stood to leave, however, Ed started talking again in a quiet, child-like voice, eyes still closed, and I sat back down. He said that when he was eight years old, he was lying in bed one night, listening to his parents talking in an adjacent room, and he heard his father say, "That boy's never going to amount to *anything*!" As soon as he said this, Ed burst into tears and sobbed uncontrollably for several minutes, obviously reliving the agony of that moment as though it had just happened. He was extremely embarrassed by this unexpected outburst and kept apologizing. I thanked him for his courage in sharing this raw experience with me, comforted and reassured him as best I could, and held his hand until he fell asleep.

Sometimes I think I know Ed's story, but all I really know is the little he shared with me about his life and the eight words from his father that he overheard when he was eight years old and still believed to be true at ninety. I'm pretty sure that it was my winsome ways that caused him to open up about his father-wound like that, but perhaps the fact that he was very old, alone, tired, in a strange place at night, literally broken, unable to even pee or poop without help, in charge of nothing for a change, and on narcotic pain medication also played a small part.

I still think about Ed after all these years. To me, he was *everyman*. It was a privilege to sit with him and to hear his story. Heck, I even got to lay some steel and fix his broken hip. I wish I could've fixed his broken heart.

Authenticity, transformation, healing, and joy
are one journey that takes us from
order through **disorder** to **reorder**,
and there are no shortcuts.

ORDER

2

Seeds

In the life of a child, order is whatever constitutes normal life as long as it's relatively safe and predictable. Like every child, I created my own safety strategy, and predictability was my father's defining trait.

My parents were from West Virginia, where my older sister and I were born. However, we grew up in Hampton, Virginia, near the coast of the Chesapeake Bay. Although we moved often, for a handful of years we lived in a house near Langley Air Force Base that I still think of as my childhood home. It was a small three-bedroom, one-bathroom ranch that one of my friends referred to as the *cracker box*.

Dad's persona was that of a Southern gentleman. In his better days, he was so sweet that sugar wouldn't melt in his mouth, and he was chock-full of Southern platitudes, bless his heart. He was utterly predictable in everything he said, even before dementia set in. My brother can do a hilarious standup routine of Dad expounding upon a variety of topics. When pressed for time, all he has to say is "conversation fourteen," and the rest of us siblings crack up because we know it by heart. I longed to have just one unscripted conversation with my father on any topic but never got the chance.

Dad had the mind of an engineer. He was a poor student in school but was very clever and could figure things out mechanically. He was always one of the "gold hat" supervisors in the construction trades and, at one time, was foreman of the maintenance department at the Hampton VA hospital. He was a master plumber and also worked as a welder and steamfitter at the local shipyard. I suspect that one of the reasons I went into orthopedic surgery was to show my dad that I inherited his mechanical genius. (I didn't.) He was a hard worker, and I remember him coming home filthy and exhausted from some of those jobs.

Dad changed jobs often as he was climbing his ladder of success, but when I was in elementary school he took a job selling life insurance at the recommendation of a family friend and stuck with it for too many years—at Mom's insistence, as I later learned. She told him that she would leave him if he quit! Unfortunately, Dad was ill-suited for this type of work, and he became depressed, irritable, and functionally disabled. As a result, our family fell into financial ruin and careened from one financial crisis to another. This was before the age of credit cards, but I saw firsthand how the poor get poorer by paying stiff penalties for having insufficient funds in the bank.

When I was ten years old, I had a bad toothache, and Mom

told Dad that I needed to see a dentist this time because aspirin and ice weren't doing the job, and I was crying. At this news, Dad started pacing back and forth across the living room, mopping his brow and yelling about not having any goddamn money to pay for a goddamn dental bill. My parents got into a shouting match about this while I just stood there crying.

I felt frightened, helpless, and ashamed for upsetting Dad like this, and I just wanted to run away and hide. Mom ended up taking me to a cut-rate dentist she'd heard about, where I had a horrendous experience. I still remember trembling and sobbing in the parking lot afterward. I didn't talk to anyone about how this experience affected me, and no one ever asked. This wasn't my last toothache, but it was the last time I let my parents know that I was hurting.

At Chez Cracker Box there was always tension in the air, and I learned to read my dad's moods at a glance. We never knew what might set Dad off. He would fly off the handle if one of us kids spilled a glass of milk at the table, so mealtimes were often tense. I grew up believing that I was a nuisance to my father, a burden, just another mouth to feed, another dental bill that he couldn't afford, another drain on his limited resources. Dad never seemed to enjoy my company, and at an early age, the harsh voice of my inner critic made its appearance and prevented me from enjoying my own company.

My older sister was a source of perpetual drama in our family, and I took on the role of her opposite: the uncomplaining, responsible, self-sufficient son. I received affirmations from Mom for this and mostly managed to stay out of Dad's line of fire by never asking for anything. For example, when I couldn't read the blackboard at school, it never even occurred to me to ask my parents for glasses. I just borrowed a pair from the kid sitting next to me and never got my own glasses until I was old enough to work and pay for them myself. I also remember signing a personal contract to pay a dental bill when I was in high school. I never received preventive or cosmetic dental care until I joined the Air Force as a married man.

Here's a verse from a poem I wrote many years ago:

> I grew up in a small house on Beverly Street,
> where I learned to pole vault and to land on my feet.
> I learned not to ask for what couldn't be had,
> and I tried really hard to not irritate Dad.

Mom was the second youngest of nine children. She grew up during the Great Depression, and her father was an abusive alcoholic from whom she was estranged for most of her life. I only met him once and never met half of her siblings. Her mother died before I was born. Mom experienced a great deal of shame at the hands of a hypercritical older sister and from a cruel aunt, with whom she was sent to live at age twelve after her parents divorced.

Nevertheless, Mom had happy memories and high hopes from her childhood. She wanted to be a dancer, movie star, or nurse when she grew up. When she was little, her older brothers would give her money to tap dance for their friends, and she was a talented singer. She even got the title role in her high school musical, *Snow White*. I remember her waltzing around the house and singing "Some Day My Prince Will Come," which never happened. Instead, she got married at eighteen, went to business school, and worked as a secretary before having children. She was twenty-two when I was born.

My mother had chronic health problems, which I'm sure is why I decided as a preschooler to become a doctor, and she always insisted that her multisystem complaints were from allergies. I don't know where she got this idea, but as I later gained knowledge in medical school, I began to question its validity. As a senior med student, I wrote a letter to the chairman of the Division of Asthma, Allergy, and Immunology at UVA, requesting an appointment for her to be seen for evaluation. My opportunity to help my mother had finally arrived!

However, the chairman wrote back denying the request for an appointment because Mom's symptoms didn't sound like allergies to him, either. His refusal to see her was extremely hurtful to my mother, and it marked the beginning of her anger and disillusionment with the traditional medical system. She was diagnosed with congestive heart failure and had a pacemaker implanted late in life, and I suspect that heart disease was the source of her symptoms all along. Ironically, I decided as a little boy to become a doctor in order to help my mom, but near the end of her life she avoided me *because* I was a doctor, and she didn't want to hear my advice to see a medical specialist for her swelling and shortness of breath.

Mom worked as a clerk-typist at a military base when she felt well enough to work. She briefly managed a beauty salon and always talked about getting her real estate license someday. During her working years, she hired a series of Black women to look after us kids when we were out of school for the summer, and I was reminded of this when I saw the 2011 movie *The Help.* However, ours wasn't a case of the rich hiring the poor; it was the poor hiring the poorer. We lived in the Jim Crow Deep South, and I can't even imagine the pittance that those poor women were paid.

Although I always felt she was on my side, my mother's limited resources were spread thinly among us five kids. I tried not to add to her burdens by taking care of myself as much as possible. As her oldest son, she depended on me in many ways as the functional man of the house and for emotional support. Mom also used illness as a means of control, one of the few that she had at her disposal. For example, she occasionally waited in the car and told me to go into local businesses to pick up bounced checks because she wasn't feeling well.

When I started dating, Mom apparently decided that the best way she could help me on my quest to become a doctor was to make sure that I didn't get waylaid by an opportunistic girlfriend, so whenever I seemed to be getting serious about someone I was dating, she expressed concerns. During my senior year of high school, she strictly forbade me to date Paula, who was unwisely open about her hopes and plans for our future together. Of course, we just sneaked around and dated anyway.

I walked and hitchhiked a lot to get around. This was pretty normal in those days, but my hitchhiking days came to an end during the mid-sixties when racial tension made it too dangerous. I also rode the city bus and sometimes splurged on a taxi if I'd scraped together a few bucks. On those rare occasions, I would sit in the back seat while closely watching the meter on the dashboard as it ticked upward. When it got close to the amount of money I had in my pocket, I'd ask the driver to pull over and would walk the rest of the way. Taxi drivers never seemed to mind this, even though I never had enough money to tip them.

I made friends easily but held friendships lightly because we moved so often. It seemed that we were always moving but never going anywhere. I went to three different schools during my four years of high school.

I detested trying to talk on the telephone because there was only one kitchen phone—no privacy—and my sister felt entitled to use it all the time. Back then, one-car families were the norm, and I found it easier to end relationships than to ask my parents for a ride to visit friends. Unfortunately, my aversion to phone calls has stuck with me all my life, and my tendency to let long-distance relationships die on the vine has only moderately improved during the last quarter-century or so.

I spent a lot of time in the woods near our house role-playing my heroes, who were all outdoorsmen like Robin Hood, Tarzan, Davy Crockett, and Daniel Boone. I built forts and teepees, practiced walking quietly like an Indian, and loved target practice with homemade spears and bows and arrows. I felt joy there. I remember looking down at my feet one day and being surprised that they were touching the ground because I felt so happy and held that I assumed I must be floating. That little patch of Sherwood Forest was my private refuge. I don't recall ever playing with friends there.

I enjoyed competitive sports and was a pretty good athlete. As I got older I joined teams and made it to practices and games in baseball, football, basketball, and track without asking my parents for anything other than permission slips. I was a pole vaulter, team captain, and MVP of the track team as a high school senior and had my career-best performance at the only meet that Dad ever came to watch. Mom never made it to any of them. I also sang in the a cappella choir, which was by far my favorite class.

There were a couple of things about growing up in the South that I didn't question at the time but give me pause now. The first is that it was considered disrespectful for a child to express anger toward a parent or other adult, so I learned to bury my anger. The second is that corporal punishment was commonly used as a disciplinary tool. *Spare the rod and spoil the child!* Dad rarely and reluctantly used his belt, usually at the end of one of those "Just wait 'til your father gets home!" days. Mom was the usual enforcer, and her weapon of choice was a switch that we kids had to procure from one of the bushes in the yard. Woe unto those who came back with a flimsy one! The pitiful bush right outside our front door was a platinum-level contributor to our education. I never felt physically abused by my parents, but now it appalls me to think that hitting a child is ever good for them.

Overall, I recall having a pretty happy childhood. This is a common statement by trauma survivors because we don't know any better as children, and we forget most of what goes on during those early years. All I had to do was stay out of trouble, be invisible, never ask for anything, go with the flow, read the room, make them laugh, keep a lid on it, and not rock the boat. *Easy peasy.* The family dynamics I grew up with were my normal and no big deal. Nevertheless, when I moved into an apartment with friends at nineteen, I was thrilled to be on my own and finally escape from all the drama. I had no idea that taking the boy out of Crazytown would be so much easier than taking Crazytown out of the boy.

I was completely unaware of the baggage I carried with me when I left home: harsh self-talk, hair-trigger sensitivity to rejection and criticism, inability to engage in conflict or share difficult feelings, compulsion to always pretend I'm okay, tendency to assume that if someone is unhappy it's probably my fault, and fierce determination to never *ever* feel like a burden to anyone. My self-created childhood survival strategy was founded upon extreme self-sufficiency and risk avoidance. Basically, if you don't ask they can't say no, and if you never let them know you're hurting they can't have a goddamn cow about how hard or inconvenient that is for them. Clearly, I was well-prepared for my first intimate relationship.

Looking back at this pivotal time in my life, I'm struck by the discrepancy between the exhilarating freedom I felt to finally be on my own, ostensibly free to live my life as I saw fit, and the reality that my future was already determined in several important ways: I was destined to always feel like a burden because that belief was planted in my mind at an early age, destined for loneliness because of my extreme secrecy and self-sufficiency, destined to parent my kids the way I was parented, and destined for physical illnesses because of my repressed anger and self-loathing. I'm beginning to understand why some people say there's no such thing as free will.

3

Cracks

Parents

Ididn't miss my family after leaving home. I had been too independent for too long to nurture those connections, and this was a source of heartache for my parents because I seldom called or visited them. Mom's phone calls were too long and exhausting, and Dad never called. I dreaded calling him on special occasions because he would almost immediately start crying and say that it was so good to *finally* hear from his children, always adding the tagline, "You'll understand someday, when you get to be my age." He did this with all of us kids, no matter how often we called, and I hated it.

Dad was the second oldest of eleven children and came from a loving family. He often said that his idea of heaven was sitting around the dinner table again with his parents and siblings, which puzzled me because sitting around the dinner table with him was no picnic. He was always rather quirky. His signature way of expressing affection was to say, "Love you a million," which was both sweet and odd. My brother and I sign our emails to each other with "LYAM."

The idea of family was very important to Dad, but this wasn't matched by any effort to engage with his own children or grandchildren. He never asked questions about my kids and would have been hard-pressed to even name them. In his later years, Dad was diagnosed with Alzheimer's disease and by the time he died he no longer recognized me. In truth, my father never knew who I was.

My parents divorced while I was in medical school, and Mom jumped from the frying pan into the fire when she married Adrian, who turned out to be cruel and abusive. Visiting Mom and "the Colonel," as she called him, always felt performative. It was hard for me to relax there, so I stayed with friends or my widowed mother-in-law whenever we were in town, which was hurtful to Mom.

I want to honor the memory of this wonderful woman who was my *good-enough* mother. She was the one I could count on as a child, who was always in my corner, made me feel loved, and modeled for me virtually every admirable trait I have. That said, Mom was very kind and generous in her younger years, but she had a hard life and eventually ran out of gas. She grew progressively bitter and controlling as she aged, which made it hard to be around her. After Adrian died and my youngest brother left home, Mom was alone, virtually housebound from agoraphobia, and nearly penniless. All of us kids pitched in to help as best we could, but there was no escape from the drama of Crazytown revisited. Perhaps mercifully, my mother died suddenly of a stroke at sixty-eight.

Marriage

Patti and I met in freshman biology lab at Christopher Newport College, and I was smitten. We had a lot in common, as we both came from lower middle-class backgrounds and were the first in our families to go to college. She, too, had an independent spirit and was working to put herself through school while living at home. We got married after our sophomore year—I was twenty-one and she was twenty—and graduated together in 1971.

I started medical school at the University of Virginia that fall. The Vietnam War was still raging, and the military was offering good deals for warm bodies, so after receiving my letter of acceptance from UVA, I made the countercultural decision to join the Air Force to pay for my medical education. It was one of the best decisions I ever made. In the meantime, Patti worked in a civil service job until our first son was born during my sophomore year.

At this time in my life, my top priority was my quest to become a doctor and achieve the American dream, bootstraps and all, and I never questioned the goodness of my desire to do this. I wanted to be a hero. I wanted to help others and also improve my own lot in life. I was quite idealistic and would have protested loudly at any suggestion that I wanted to acquire power or wealth. I figured I'd end up living in a jungle somewhere—compassionate, brilliant, humble, poor, discoverer of the cure for some terrible disease, and revered by the world. I especially enjoyed thinking about being revered by the world.

I believed that Patti should adjust her goals, career, schedule, and dreams to satisfy mine and that she should willingly leave her job, friends, and family to move whenever and wherever my schooling, career, or sense of longing dictated. When she complained, which was remarkably seldom, my trump card was to point out that my advancement along my chosen path would eventually lead to a better quality of life for her. The partner of a young man on his heroic journey could really use the counsel of a wise mentor!

I don't wish to lay a guilt trip on anyone working hard and trying to get ahead and provide for their family. I just think back to all the years of my medical school and residency training, when Patti had to do so much of the domestic heavy lifting—years when I wasn't around to help out with the kids and do countless other things that a husband and father should do. Would I have compassionately listened to her and seriously considered altering the path of my lifelong quest to become a doctor if she had pushed back? No way. I would have undoubtedly become defensive and resentful instead.

Patti discovered early in our marriage that she couldn't tell me how she felt when she was upset with me because I became extremely defensive. Nevertheless, we got along well most of the time because we had similar values, we respected and loved each other, and I avoided conflict like the plague. I had to be handled with care, but Patti had a soft touch that enabled her to usually work around my many sensitivities.

When stressed, I found it a bit harder to run away and play in the woods as a husband and father than it had been as a boy. Instead, as a medical student, I learned to play guitar and spent much of my free time hanging out with Peter, Paul, and Mary. I continued my secretive ways, and the seeds of loneliness that had been sown during childhood began to take root.

In my late twenties, I was stationed in England for three years as a flight surgeon, which is basically a family doctor for the fliers and their dependents. I was also on flight status and flew with an F-111 fighter squadron. Two of our kids were born in England, so we arrived there with one son and returned home with three. During this self-chosen extended break between my internship and residency, my work schedule was light enough that I was able to occasionally sing and play guitar with friends at coffee shop gatherings and talent shows.

While in England, Patti and I attended a Catholic-affiliated Marriage Encounter retreat that breathed new life into our marriage. For the first time, I heard the message that positive or negative, feelings are always valid. What really helped me was the introduction of a communication technique called Dialogue, in which a couple writes daily letters to each other that are focused on sharing feelings. We took turns choosing the question for our letter du jour, always prefaced by "What are my feelings when . . ." or "How do I feel about . . ."

After writing in separate rooms, we got together, read each other's letters twice—once for the head and once for the heart—and talked about whatever came up. Dialogue gave me an important degree of separation to begin expressing my feelings. I could be much more open and honest when writing in a separate room than I had ever been able to do in face-to-face conversations, and for the first time in my life, I began to experience emotional intimacy. It was liberating.

We kept up our daily letter-writing routine and also hosted Marriage Encounter meetings for a long time, but then life happened. We weren't able to maintain the required discipline, and I settled back into my old habits. Dialogue probably extended the life of our marriage, but I could never take the next step of talking in real time about my deepest feelings, needs, and desires—especially the ones that felt too risky or selfish.

According to Brené Brown, vulnerability is the key to unlocking intimacy, and it always involves risk, uncertainty, and emotional exposure. Furthermore, you can't "do" vulnerability by yourself. This is very bad news for hardcore conflict avoiders and pathologically self-sufficient men such as myself, and it put a great deal of pressure on the bedroom to fulfill all of my intimacy needs. This is a common scenario with men.

If you're playing a word association game and the first word is *intimacy*, I'll wager that 90 percent of men will respond with *sex*, and the other 10 percent have probably never heard the word. The sex drive in a young man is a force of nature on par with a Category 5 hurricane, and even old men are buffeted by gale-force winds. We can thank this hormonally driven compulsion for the survival of our species, but let's be honest here: The penis-driven life is just too much, even in its more benign manifestations.

One of the main reasons that most men get married is to enjoy an active sexual relationship with their beloved, so there's a lot riding on how that goes. Unfortunately, most men find sexual relationships to be difficult. Franciscan priest and best-selling author Richard Rohr says that he has never had a man tell him that he felt his sexuality was whole, healthy, and happy.

The fact that father-wounding and sexual-wounding are both ubiquitous among men is no coincidence. They go hand in hand because vulnerability makes trauma survivors feel extremely unsafe. What is it like to feel this way? For me, it's like standing on a platform high in the air and being asked to step out onto a surface that I know won't support me. It's like standing in half an inch of water and thinking, *I'm going to drown!*

I remember the first time, as a young newlywed, that I asked Patti to have sex with me, and she turned me down. There was nothing remarkable about this incident except for the fact that I was suddenly overwhelmed with deep feelings of shame, fear, and helplessness. I was triggered into re-experiencing the trauma of my toothache story, but this was the first time that I had ever experienced a flashback, and I didn't know what hit me. I wasn't able to connect the dots for many years, but this incident fundamentally changed our marriage. After that, I struggled mightily to reconcile my Category 5 desire with fear of drowning.

From my point of view, the obvious solution would've been for my wife to take a course in mind reading and take a pill to pump up her sex drive. This would have left intact my childhood program of hoping to get what I want without ever having to ask for it. Unfortunately, I'm not great at changing programs, which is why it took me forever to upgrade from Windows 7 to Windows 10. I still have nightmares about that.

On high alert now, I soldiered on, but courage turns out to be a greater asset on the battlefield than in the bedroom. I found it best to bide my time until all of the signs were positive, which was seldom, especially after we started having children. Through careful risk avoidance, I never experienced another flashback in our twenty-year marriage, and I never talked to Patti about any of this.

Children

One of my sons has had anger issues from the time he was a toddler. He would often fly off the handle with seemingly no provocation. Where was this coming from? After all, I was a laid-back dad who was engaged with my children and enjoyed their company—precisely the opposite of my father—so I was always baffled by my son's anger.

When I was in my early sixties, I visited him during a time of upheaval in his personal life. I watched my son trying very hard to be a good dad to his two little boys at a time when they were acting out their stress with loud and defiant behavior, and I was struck by the discrepancy between my son's affirming words and his nonverbal language of irritation with them. The evening before I flew home, we all went to a restaurant, where my grandsons' behavior was disruptive to the other patrons. I remembered how I had felt and behaved as a young father when my own sons had misbehaved in public places, and I didn't like it.

I was lying in bed that night when my feelings and observations from the previous few days fell into place in a moment of insight. I finally understood why my son was so angry as a child: I wounded him with my nonverbal messages of irritation, just like my father had wounded me. I realized that I wasn't the laid-back dad I always thought I was. Instead, I was a hyper-vigilant disciplinarian who was hell-bent on keeping my children—an extension of me—from ever being a burden to others, and I was blind to my lack of attunement to my son's inner world. He, on the other hand, was very sensitive to my nonverbal language of irritation. He could never be a good enough boy to make his daddy happy, and that royally pissed him off.

I spent some time alone with my son before leaving that day, and I shared my observations with him. I asked him if I had wounded him in this way as a child, and after a few minutes of quietly thinking about it, he confirmed my suspicion. He talked about how painful it was for him to have a hypercritical hockey coach, even though he was co-captain and MVP of their state championship team, and how powerfully he had related to the boy in *Dead Poets Society* who could never please his father.

He also talked about the scene in *Good Will Hunting*, when Robin Williams told Matt Damon over and over in a breakthrough moment of therapy, "It's not your fault . . . It's not your fault . . ." I realized that despite his lifelong anger issues, my son has never once said anything to me personally that was mean or hurtful. Obviously, what I think of him has always been extremely important to him. I don't know why I didn't pick up on the significance of that earlier.

Oh man, so many years of missed opportunities to affirm the incredible goodness in my beautiful son! We both started crying as we talked, and it still makes me cry to think about it. I told him how very sorry I was, that he has always been an absolute joy for me, and that my irritability and lack of attunement weren't his fault. He told me that he forgives me, doesn't blame me for his anger, and takes full responsibility for his behavior. I suggested that he rewatch those movies and journal about his memories and feelings. A few months later, he flew out to Wisconsin, and we spent a wonderful weekend together at a cabin, where our focus was bringing healing to my son's father-wound and our relationship.

All three of my older sons experienced the same thing with me: preoccupation with whatever was going on in my life, frequent lack of attunement to what was going on in theirs, and chronic irritability. Later, I received further confirmation of my behavior as a young dad when I watched an old video of me playing football with my sons in the backyard. I always remembered this as a fun time, but the video showed otherwise. My sons were running around just acting like kids, while I was obviously irritated with them the whole time.

Father-wounding is a multigenerational chain of trauma, within which each link firmly believes that he broke the chain. For most of my life, I was convinced that I was nothing like my dad. If you're feeling really brave, ask your wife and kids if this is true for you.

Seeking

My parents taught me early in life to put my trust in the invisible Jesus, but my first practical experience of faith in a higher power was my belief in Santa Claus. He wasn't just an idea. Santa came to my house every Christmas and left presents he had picked out specially for me! I was a true believer in Santa for years beyond the normal age of enlightenment about such things, especially after I saw on TV that his sled had been picked up on radar by NASA, which was located right down the road from where I lived. Modern technology confirmed my faith!

Then one year, I overheard Mom talking about Christmas and

I said something that made her pause, get a funny look on her face, and ask, "You don't still believe in Santa, do you?"

It was a reasonable question, given that I had a full beard and was eligible to vote by then. I just scoffed and said, too convincingly, "Of course not!" before running to my room and crying my eyes out. I would never again be so gullible.

I was raised in the Church of the Brethren, a conservative Christian denomination in which my grandfather was a pastor, but I lost interest in religion from my teens until I was living in England in my late twenties. That's where I met Phil, an overweight Pentecostal preacher, talented baritone, and jet aircraft mechanic from the Deep South who had an annoying habit of honking mid-sentence to clear his sinuses. For some reason, I started going to church with Phil and reading the Bible.

I recall sitting on the stairs at home, reading with astonishment from the Acts of the Apostles about the miracles that occurred on the day of Pentecost—miracles that continue to this day, according to Pentecostals, if you just have enough faith. How had I missed that when I was growing up in my church?

I loved the idea of a living Spirit who interacts with us, answers prayers, and suffuses everyday life with power and meaning, and I was only mildly put off by people speaking in tongues. However, I was pretty uncomfortable with the drama of people being "slain in the Spirit," miraculous healings of questionable authenticity, and the certainty among Pentecostals that there are no coincidences. In their world, the Holy Spirit regularly intervened to solve a host of practical problems, like fixing a broken refrigerator. That's why, to this day, I never complain when someone cuts in front of me to steal a parking space at the mall. Heck, they might be a Pentecostal, and who am I to thwart the will of the Holy Spirit?

Despite my reservations, it was a powerful draw, and I tried my very best to muster up enough faith to become one of them—without success, as it turned out. I fasted, surrendered, tried really hard, tried not trying, asked to be filled with the Holy Spirit, and was prayed over by brothers and sisters who were obviously very close to God. On some nights, alone in the call room at the hospital, I sat on the floor with a candle, fervently asked God to give me a small but unequivocal sign of His presence, and promised that it would just be our little secret, *wink-wink.*

It doesn't take a genius to see the parallel relationships I had with my earthly and heavenly fathers, and I suspect that many people with father-wounds struggle with divine masculine images. I wanted more than anything to experience God's presence, not just believe it intellectually, but all I ever experienced was His holy and righteous lack of interest. After years of fruitless searching, I finally concluded that there's either something terribly wrong with me or these people are bonkers—probably both.

I eventually joined the Catholic church because Patti was a lifelong Catholic, and we thought it would be good for our children to grow up with parents who go to church together and are on the same page spiritually. Soon after becoming a Catholic, I attended a Cursillo weekend retreat, an invitation-only program designed to deepen the spiritual journey and facilitate community participation with other like-minded men.

I enjoyed hanging out with a bunch of good guys, but the retreat did nothing for me spiritually. At the conclusion, there was a gathering of family and friends to celebrate this milestone event, and all of the attendees (except me) came up front, one at a time, to share stories of how they had experienced God's presence. There was a pregnant pause after everyone else had spoken, and I was embarrassed by having nothing to say.

I was bored by the insipid homilies at Mass, offended by a priest who made a sexual pass at me, and never really felt at home as a Catholic-come-lately Protestant convert. Nevertheless, my all-time peak church experience occurred while I was a Catholic. One Sunday, a conservatively dressed elderly man walked up front to read a passage from the Old Testament that had something to do with Israel's battles with the surrounding pagan tribes. The man got through the Jebusites without difficulty, but when he came to the Hittites, he pronounced them "High Titties" in a clear, booming voice. The poor guy must've said High Titties a half-dozen times, and I almost wet myself. That's when I knew in my heart that there is a God, and She has a sense of humor. Nevertheless, my thirst for an experience of God's presence remained unquenched by the time I hit my mid-thirties, and that's when things started to fall apart in my life.

DISORDER

4

Hands

The first thing I remember is standing at the scrub sink in the operating room at the Air Force Academy Hospital and noticing that the tops of my wrists were swollen and squishy. I asked Dan, who was scrubbing at the sink next to mine, what he thought, but he wasn't impressed. Just three months earlier, I had finally completed four years of medical school and five years of residency training to become an orthopedic surgeon, and I was just starting my career at age thirty-six. Despite Dan's assurance, standing at that sink was when I first knew in my gut that this was not going to go well.

My symptoms rapidly progressed over the next couple of months. My wrists and hands became warm, swollen, and tender, and it hurt to shake hands or use a power grip, which is often required during orthopedic procedures. When I straightened and bent my fingers, you could hear the tendons squeaking from across the room, like a rusty hinge. I tried self-medicating with aspirin and ibuprofen without benefit. My primary care provider referred me to a rheumatologist, who happened to be the hospital commander.

The rheumatologist did some blood work, which was normal, and he gave me a diagnosis of "idiopathic seronegative rheumatoid arthritis," which is medical-speak for, "You definitely have arthritis, but your tests are all negative, and we have no idea what caused it." This is a familiar conversation for anyone diagnosed with an autoimmune disease. He put me on prescription medication, but it didn't help. Neither did the next medication, or the one after that.

I started seeing an occupational therapist, who gave me night splints and a tinker-toy-like "hand gym" for exercises. Within a few months, I could no longer play my beloved guitar but could still do my job with some difficulty. My rheumatologist thought I should consider doing another residency in a specialty that didn't require so much hand strength—maybe radiology. This option was uniquely available to me because I was on active duty and wouldn't suffer an income loss while retraining. But, *Whoa, hold on there, sir, ANOTHER RESIDENCY? ARE YOU FUCKING SERIOUS?* This crisis of limitation was the first time I had ever encountered a problem that I couldn't overcome by simply working harder. The tightly wound ball of string that had been my life until then began to unravel.

I was angry at God for pulling the rug on me, but desperate for relief, so one night I went to a Christian healing service at a nearby church. I sat in the audience for a while and watched the guest preacher lay on hands and pray for healing, as a line of desperate people slowly snaked forward. However, I walked out halfway through the show, chiding myself for not being brave enough to go up on stage and stupid enough to be there in the first place.

Next, I went to see a holistic practitioner. She was very cautious at first, convinced that I was a traditional MD who just wanted to debunk her genre of care. She measured my energy fields while I held various foods in my hand and prescribed what seemed like a thousand dietary supplements that took up all of our kitchen counter space at home. However, they only caused hot flashes and gave my poop a disturbingly beautiful hue. As a traditionally trained surgeon, this didn't make a lick of sense to me, but nothing did anymore, and I kept coming back to see her. By then, I had failed standard treatment, had nothing to lose, and was pretty much open to all options.

During the next year, this woman and I gradually became good friends. One day, she asked if I would be interested in doing a healing ceremony, and I said yes. We met early in the morning at Garden of the Gods, an awe-inspiring park in the foothills of Colorado Springs, and found a secluded spot for the ceremony. She wore Native attire, blessed the space with sage, did some quiet drumming and chanting, and took my hands in hers as she prayed for healing. The ceremony took place about two years after the onset of my symptoms, and within two weeks the swelling and pain disappeared completely from my wrists and hands.

The inflammatory phase of my arthritis had burned out, but by then, so had my faith in God and enthusiasm for the lonely life I was living. I no longer had pain and was still quite functional, so

I was very grateful for the improvement. Gradually, I even let go of my fear of doing another residency. However, I had hoped for a complete return to normal, and it took a long time to accept that I had permanent stiffness and deformity, especially in the fingers of my right hand. Over the next few years I had several minor operations for trigger fingers, which resulted from the previous inflammation in the tendon sheaths. In addition, I had to figure out a few mechanical techniques to work around my loss of grip strength at work. By necessity, I learned to adapt to unwelcome realities over which I had no control.

Everyone who gets a serious disease has so many questions: *Why this? Why now? Why me?* I wondered if my arthritis might be the physical manifestation of a hidden psychological problem. Did I wake up with a clenched fist every day because of repressed anger?

Pain that's not transformed is always transmitted, typically to our families, but it doesn't stop there. Our bodies also keep the score. There is compelling evidence, advanced by scientists from many fields, that an intimate relationship exists between the brain and the immune system. An individual's emotional makeup and response to chronic stress are highly correlated with the onset and clinical course of many diseases, including the entire spectrum of autoimmune diseases that can affect the joints, muscles, skin, digestive tract, and nervous system. There is a finely tuned interdependence of emotions and physiology in health and illness, down to the cellular level.

Many people with rheumatoid arthritis have the following traits, acquired early in life: non-complaining hyper-stoicism, ignored emotional needs, extreme independence, belief that they can and must get through everything by themselves, role reversal with a parent, early actual or functional loss of one or both parents, perfectionism, denial of anger and hostility, strong feelings of inadequacy, and anger toward a parent or other attachment figure redirected inward, causing inappropriate self-criticism.

Well, damn! I always thought I was the healthy kid in my family. I was responsible, adaptable, a hard worker, and peacemaker—traits that most parents would love to see in their children—but I wasn't healthy. I had just learned to bury my needs and feelings in order to survive in a dysfunctional family environment. (Note to parents: Worry about your excessively "good" kids. The hell-raisers will probably turn out okay if they survive into adulthood.)

Babies aren't born with the ability to hide their emotions. They'd never survive without making their needs known, loudly and clearly. Any childhood safety and survival program that's based upon pretense and repression of feelings is learned behavior in response to stress that will likely lead to sickness if it persists into adulthood.

Was this the source of my arthritis? I'll never know for sure, but it seems extremely likely that decades of pretending to be okay was a key factor in my hands manifesting undeniable evidence that I really wasn't. It also seems likely that my close friendship with the woman who performed the healing ceremony was an important factor in the resolution of inflammation in my hands.

There is overwhelming evidence that psychological and social factors, including childhood trauma, play a huge role in the development and clinical course of many diseases. However, our prevailing biomedical model largely fails to take this into account, and I don't see much evidence that things have changed in the half-century since I was a medical student.

Medical and surgical specialists still look at everything through the narrow lenses of our areas of expertise, and primary care providers are simply too busy to explore the mind-body connection, even if they're interested. Time is money in a fee-for-service healthcare system such as ours, and only so much can be done in a fifteen-minute appointment. Patients don't like to be kept waiting, and physician income is often tied to patient satisfaction scores. In many medical groups, physicians must also meet patient-contact quotas in order to remain in good standing. To our detriment, there remains a big divide between the world of physicians and surgeons and that of mental health professionals. They all do what they do quite well, but never the twain shall meet in our current system.

My hands weren't ready to retire from the teaching profession. In my mid-forties, I developed splitting of the skin on both hands due to psoriasis. They looked and felt like they were covered in paper cuts, especially during the winter, and I live in Wisconsin. After trying a gazillion treatments, I settled on superglue. (Helpful hint: Make sure it's dry before touching anything.) This was the second autoimmune disease to manifest itself in my hands.

It's not a small thing to ask a newly diagnosed patient to explore their important relationships as a possible factor in the development of a disease, but I needn't have worried. Despite having two autoimmune diseases, no medical doctor has ever asked me what was going on in my life that might be stressful. *Whew! Awkward two-minute conversations with my rheumatologist and dermatologist averted!*

I'm being facetious here, but barely. Despite so much evidence for the mind-body connection in health and illness, in my experience, most patients become defensive if asked too many probing questions about possible psychological and social factors when they see a doctor for physical complaints. *He thinks this is all in my head!* The body keeps the score while the mind denies responsibility.

5

Transitions

It's hard to be in longstanding pain without blaming someone, and spouses are commonly the recipients of that dubious honor. In my late thirties, arthritis had rocked my world, and things were falling apart, so I attempted to solve that problem by bushwhacking my way to a destination that was teeming with middle-aged men: I had an extramarital affair, got my own apartment, and filed for divorce. *Boom!* Just like that. I had never threatened divorce, suggested that we see a marriage counselor, or even let on that I was so unhappy. My sons were 13, 9, and 8, and my daughter was a baby. Forty years later, it still shocks me to know that I did such an awful thing. (More on this in Chapter 8.)

People who have affairs often tell stories of recent losses that made them question long-held beliefs and priorities, and arthritis certainly checked that box for me. Furthermore, if you have trouble accessing intimacy, as I did, you will sometimes reach out for it in very unhealthy ways that hurt other people because intimacy is a thirst that *will* be quenched, even if it's with poison. I was not aware of these factors in my decision-making at the time. I just felt like I was dying.

The best way to describe what happened to my family is that a life-as-you-know-it-ending bomb went off in all of their lives. This was shocking to everyone who knew us and incomprehensible to Patti and the kids, who had rarely even seen us argue. For the next eight months, I spent as much time as possible with our children, who acted out their distress in various ways. Then I moved from Colorado Springs to Salt Lake City for fellowship training in pediatric orthopedic surgery. This assignment had been in the pipeline for a couple of years, and I didn't have the option to leave the Air Force or stay in Colorado Springs because of my military obligation. The day I drove away was seared into the minds of my children, and I took on the hellish role of long-distance parenting, flying back and forth as often as I could.

I briefly dated several women while in Utah, but my life was in turmoil, and I had nothing to offer anyone who might be looking for a long-term, healthy relationship. I had a wonderful training experience at the university but missed my kids terribly, and it was the hardest, loneliest year of my life. From there I was assigned to Wright-Patterson Air Force Base in Dayton, Ohio, where I finished my twenty-year military career and settled into my new version of normal life. After retiring from the Air Force I took a job in Richmond, Virginia, but wasn't busy enough. So in 1993 I joined a multispecialty group in Madison, Wisconsin, where I've lived ever since.

The second half of my life did not begin well. I was a divorced, long-distance father of four, living on a shoestring budget, and my life was a soap opera of anger, guilt, and despair. I was ashamed to see people who knew my story, so I cut off contact with pretty much everyone from my previous life. I was terribly lonely and hung out with Jack Daniels in the evenings when not on call. I decided that this would be a terrific time to remarry.

I don't normally recommend divorce and remarriage as a tool of self-discovery. Still, if you're going to do it anyway, you might as well learn what it has to teach you, and it quickly became obvious that I was struggling with the same issues I had struggled with in my first marriage and dealing with them in the same dysfunctional ways. The only consistent link in my chain of broken relationships was . . . me! I had jumped from the frying pan into the fire, and the happiness that my family and I had paid an enormous price to find was nowhere to be found. For the foreseeable future, it would take an Oscar-worthy performance to continue pretending to be okay.

One of the things that I found most attractive about Lori is that she's a truth-teller, but I soon discovered that truth-tellers don't feel the need to tiptoe around other people's feelings. My minefield of sensitivities was by now the size of Chernobyl. What I mainly remember about that period of time is the *OMG!* experience. The combination of my thin skin and Lori's style of truth-telling triggered flashbacks fairly often, which caused me to shut down and withdraw into my silent tower of self-sufficiency. This is precisely the way I felt and responded when my dad was irritated with me as a child, but I couldn't connect the dots between the present and the past because there was a "hook" that kept me from seeing my role in my difficult marriage.

The hook was that Lori doesn't, in fact, have a natural soft touch, so it was easy to point the finger of blame at her and exonerate myself from any role in our relationship struggles. I needed to work with her in real time on how to talk to me, not just complain about it days later, but I could never do this because my flashbacks shut down my ability to talk. I needed to get healthier before I could transition from Lori's critic to her partner in working through our communication issues.

I loved Lori as much as I was capable of loving anyone, but after a few years of marriage, I was really struggling to hang in there. As was my way, I privately weighed my options, no longer naive about the consequences of the choices I was considering, and decided to stay in my marriage, do the best I could, hope for better days, and at least become a man who kept his promises. I quietly exchanged my fruitless pursuit of happiness for the pursuit of integrity.

So I sat down with Lori one day and told her that I would never leave her, always be faithful, and always do my best to show her my love. She appreciated what I had to say but wondered where this was coming from. Um, hadn't I promised these things on our wedding day? Lori didn't know I was so unhappy because—yep, you guessed it—I'm a skilled and experienced pretender.

Looking back, this private recommitment to our marriage was the lackluster beginning of my healing journey. It provided a sanctuary where I could practice being real without worrying that my inevitable mistakes were deal-breakers. After all, you can't risk being honest about who you are and what's really going on in your life unless you know that no matter how your effort turns out today, you and your partner will come back tomorrow to try again. I always knew that Lori would come back. Now I knew that I would, too, no matter what.

Making promises on your wedding day is one thing, but doing it from the pits is when you find out how serious you really are, and I had a lousy track record from my first marriage. I found my renewed commitment to be both comforting and scary, for it gave me a much-needed port in the storm and a safe container within which to get started on some sort of major self-improvement project, details to be determined. Seriously, if I'd known what to do, I wouldn't have been in this pickle in the first place.

For those who grew up feeling unworthy of love, my advice is to go to medical school because the next best thing is to feel needed—a gateway drug to workaholism for many people in the helping professions. Over the next dozen years, I mostly put one foot in front of the other, took care of my responsibilities, and got through the day. I also learned to compartmentalize my life. At work, I enjoyed the perks and privileges of being a surgeon, which kept my tank from running dry. These perks included respect from colleagues, daily doses of banter with coworkers, and expressions of gratitude from patients and their families.

At home, I was often depressed and sought solace in the fridge and pantry, acquired a taste for red wine, and got fat. There is always trauma in the lives of people who have an addiction. My kids started expressing concerns about my health, so I took a weight reduction class in which I was the only male, *duh*, and joined a gym, which I rarely visited. I managed to stay afloat but was never a good swimmer.

I wanted to shed my defensiveness and open my heart to

Lori, but I didn't know how. This is a common struggle with trauma survivors. I remembered learning about constrictive pericarditis in medical school, a condition in which a thickening of the normally thin, sac-like membrane around the heart can interfere with cardiac function. "When all you have is a scalpel, everything looks like an operation," as the old saying goes, so I decided to create a surgical ritual to deal with this problem.

I went out of town for a couple of days, taking with me a stone heart I had purchased and slathered on multiple layers of papier mâché. After the layers dried, I prayerfully performed a ritual of cutting away the papier mâché, hoping it would enable my real heart to beat freely with love for my wife. However, I experienced no lasting benefit.

At my suggestion, Lori and I went to see a therapist about our sexual relationship. I wish I could've talked about why the bedroom was not a safe place for me, how fear of rejection robbed me of humor and self-confidence, and especially where all of that came from, but I just wanted to talk about frequency. Lori tried her best to partner with me on this and other related issues, but it was never enough to satisfy me, and I was always on high alert.

I thought not enough sex was the simple problem and more sex the simple solution, but father-wounding creates an insatiable desire for *more* to make up for all that you supposedly lack: more sex, money, power, respect, attention, praise, titles, safety—you name it. I'm reminded of my patient, Ed, who, at ninety, was still haunted by his father's prediction that he would never amount to anything despite being wildly successful in his career. There wasn't enough success in the world to fill the hole in that man's soul and not enough sex in the world to fill the hole in mine.

It seems to me that childhood trauma, rather than sin or ego, accounts for most of the adult behavior we attribute to our false self, or mistaken identity. *What I have, what I do,* and *what others think of me* are the expected preoccupations of someone trying to fill a hole in their soul.

When one of my sons was in his early twenties, he was admitted to a rehab facility for substance use disorder. After he got through detox, I flew out to visit him and sat in on several of his twelve-step meetings, where I witnessed raw honesty for the first time. When it came time to leave, I was heartbroken for my son's suffering and deeply worried about his future, but at the same time I didn't want to leave because I was so inspired by the courageous truth-telling that I witnessed in those broken men and women.

This visit was a milestone event in my own healing journey. In contrast with the truth-telling that I witnessed in those meetings, for the first time I saw clearly, as in a mirror, the magnitude, pervasiveness, and fruits of my own lack of honesty. Pretending to be okay all the time sounds rather benign, but it's a soul-crushing survival strategy. Deep down, I wanted to be known and loved for who I really was, and by midlife, this desire had become a clanging imperative. As a result of my experience at the rehab center, radical authenticity became a goal toward which I began to slowly and fearfully crawl.

6

The T-Word

Carl was my best friend and teammate on our little league baseball team, and he lived in my neighborhood, so we hung out together all the time. One afternoon, we were playing at my house when he suddenly remembered that his dad had told him to burn the pile of leaves in their backyard before he got home from work. His dad was not known for his patience, so Carl ran home to get the job done.

The ground was wet, however, and Carl couldn't get the fire started, so he threw some gasoline on the smoldering pile of leaves to help things along. The gas can exploded, and Carl ran into his house engulfed in flames. His mom threw him to the floor and beat out the fire with her hands, sustaining severe burns herself, but Carl was mortally wounded. He stayed in the ICU for two weeks before dying, and I never got to visit him. I'm sure that my parents wanted to protect me from seeing my horribly disfigured friend, but I never got to say goodbye to Carl and didn't even realize how critically he was injured until they told me that he had died.

I was inconsolable for many weeks and remember pouring out my heart in prayer night after night, begging for a miracle of resurrection or to exchange my life for Carl's. I was angry at God for allowing this to happen, angry at my parents for not taking me to see him, and filled with shame for making him late on that fateful day. When something terrible happens to you as a child, you assume it's because you're a terrible person.

Carl was the catcher and best player on our baseball team, and at the end of the season he would have undoubtedly been one of the three players from our team chosen as all-stars. However, I made the all-star team that year and felt that I had stolen that honor from Carl. I didn't get close enough to anyone to call them my best friend for the next half century.

The word *trauma* comes from the Greek word for *wound* and originally referred only to physical wounding, but the definition today also includes deep emotional wounding that is caused by a profoundly disturbing event or series of events. Not everyone is comfortable with this expanded definition, however, and most people still use the word only with newsworthy events such as combat, catastrophic accidents, and physical or sexual assault. Hurtful words, regardless of their impact, don't usually make the cut. I'm sure that Ed wouldn't have used the T-word to describe what he experienced as an eight-year-old, yet there he was at ninety, sobbing at the memory of it.

Words like *trauma* and *father-wound* seem to point the finger of blame at parents whom we love and don't wish to accuse of wrongdoing, and this reluctance can be a barrier to our own healing. Parent-wounding is almost always multigenerational; no one really knows where it began, and it's nobody's fault. We know so little about the day-to-day lives of our parents when they were children, much less the lives of our grandparents and beyond. What events in their lives had consequences that were unintentionally passed on to us? We'll never know, just as our descendants will likely never know the parts of our story that we passed on to them, for good and for ill.

In a sense, we are all trauma survivors, having lived through the inevitable wounds and losses of childhood, and we get through most of them fine and learn valuable lessons along the way. However, trauma isn't what happens to you; it's what happens inside as a result of what happens to you. After some heart-wrenching events, our world is experienced with a different nervous system that continues to flood us with intolerable emotions and physical reactions. It becomes impossible to coordinate our feelings with our thinking, and we have a very hard time living in the present, experiencing pleasure, figuring out the intricacies of successful relationships, and dealing with the normal disappointments and frustrations of life.

Children don't get traumatized because they're hurt. They get traumatized because they're alone with their pain, and having a calm and empathetic parent or other adult to talk to afterward can greatly diminish the impact of trauma. I'm sure that my toothache story wouldn't have been so impactful if I'd had someone to talk to about it afterward, but Dad was the source of the trauma, Mom was traumatized as well, and there were no other safe adults around.

Trauma experts sometimes divide trauma into large-T and small-t categories, with childhood trauma typically consisting of a series of painful but outwardly undramatic events that take place over years. Most traumatized children don't meet the diagnostic criteria for PTSD, and this has led many mental health professionals to join forces in recommending a new diagnostic category for children: developmental trauma disorder.

Childhood trauma covers a broad spectrum of events, each of which has a broad range of possible consequences that are manifested differently during the childhood and adult years of an individual. That's a lot of moving parts. Although it's an oversimplification, I find it useful to think in terms of large-T and small-t trauma events having large-C or small-c consequences in people's lives. Accordingly, Ed appears to have experienced large-C consequences as the result of his small-t childhood trauma, as did I, and this is typically the case with garden-variety father-wounding.

In case you're wondering about an example of small-t trauma with small-c consequences, here's one that comes to mind: When I was in eighth-grade health class, our uber-sensitive football coach was droning on about the physical changes of adolescence one day while walking up and down the aisles in our classroom, when he suddenly stopped next to my desk and said—nay, yelled at the top of his lungs for all sentient beings to stop whatever they were doing and listen intently— "I'll bet by the end of the day you could get a teaspoon of oil off of Keith's face!"

I wore a bag over my head for the rest of that school year, but

I eventually recovered from this trauma with only compulsive face-washing and a strong aversion to skin creams, including sunscreen, as residual symptoms. If I ever get skin cancer, I'll upgrade to large-C and go pee on Coach's grave. Just kidding. Maybe. He's buried in Tuscaloosa, Alabama. I looked it up.

Childhood trauma has a spectrum of severity that impacts our relational and mental health as adults, and there is objective evidence for this in the form of the Adverse Childhood Experiences (ACE) Study, a landmark survey in the 1990s of nearly seventeen thousand Kaiser Permanente HMO patients. The study consisted of just ten probing questions about incidents of physical, emotional, and sexual trauma or abuse (including witnessing or being the victim), being in the presence of an adult who abused alcohol or drugs, and familial mental health. ACE testing is now commonly used in medical practices as a screening tool.

The ACE Study proved conclusively that bad stuff in childhood—including family violence, neglect, abuse, chaos, poverty, abandonment, loneliness, drug use, and alcoholism—begets really bad stuff in adulthood, and the more affirmative responses to the ten ACE questions, the greater is the likelihood that a child will grow into an adult with significant mental health problems.

For example, people with ACE scores of four or higher are twenty times more likely to be incarcerated at some point in their lives than the general population. ACE scores of seven or more are associated with a fifty-one-fold increase in suicide attempts among adolescents and a thirty-fold increase among adults. Even a score of one is associated with a marked increase in adult alcoholism, depression, and divorce.

ACE screening is a powerful tool for assessing the population impact of childhood trauma, but it fails to take into account the large-C consequences that years of small-t trauma events can have with father-wounding. Furthermore, it's not a diagnostic tool, nor is it predictive for an individual, with this caveat: If either you or your partner had a substantially adverse childhood, it doesn't necessarily mean that you won't be able to enjoy a healthy relationship, but it'll take a lot of work by both of you for that to happen. The wounded partner must be willing and able to face their demons and will likely need skilled help to do so. If both of you had substantially adverse childhoods, well, my advice is to strap on your crash helmets and fasten your seatbelts because you're in for a rough ride.

These are sobering realities, but we have an astonishing capacity to heal, physically and emotionally, and it's not by sheer willpower or brute force. We have unseen legions that fight our battles for us and never sleep. One of the gifts of being a surgeon is that I've seen it a thousand times, and I never cease to be amazed by the healing power of mutually vulnerable love relationships.

Never feeling good enough and broken relationships aren't front-page news, but the cumulative effect of a lifetime of hidden and denied suffering can be the equivalent of an eight-year-old stepping on a landmine. Years ago, I treated a child from Nicaragua who had his leg blown off when he stepped on a mine that was left over from their Civil War. He survived but with a permanent and pronounced limp.

Ed's "limp" was also debilitating but harder to detect because it consisted of family conflicts that were hidden behind closed doors and feelings of never amounting to anything that were buried beneath a boatload of career accomplishments. These were his Band-Aids, which can temporarily cover a festering wound but never heal it. The tipoff is that with unhealed trauma, you never have enough Band-Aids.

One of the fundamental principles of orthopedic wound care applies equally well to emotional trauma: the imperative to thoroughly explore a fresh wound. A tiny cut in the skin might be the only external sign of a deep injury. However, a patient in the emergency department doesn't want the doctor to poke around to see what's inside because wound exploration is painful. It can be tempting to just wash the skin, maybe throw in a couple of sutures, and cover the wound with a bandage, but deep wounds that are managed superficially often develop dangerous abscesses. Unexplored physical and emotional wounds tend to fester and cause serious long-term problems.

Because I'm an orthopedic surgeon, men usually feel comfortable asking my opinion about their swollen knees and sore shoulders, especially sports injuries, which are often a badge of honor among men. However, I'm pretty sure that those same men would never ask for my curbside opinion about their depression, anxiety, or marital struggles if I were a shrink, and I'd be in no danger of being corralled in the locker room by a man who just wants to chat about his father-wound. To our detriment, men talk openly about physical injuries but deal with emotional trauma alone and in silence.

Despite the near-universal resistance to using the word *trauma* with our own small-t stories, there are several good reasons to do so. First, it changes your mindset from *What's wrong with me?* to *What happened to me?* This shift can be quite liberating because it replaces a shaming message with one of self-compassion. Also, whenever you have an emotional reaction, an old wound is being triggered, and once you realize this about yourself, the same obviously applies to everyone else. Your mindset with difficult people begins to shift from *What the hell is wrong with her?* to *I wonder what happened to her.* A trauma-informed society is a kinder and gentler one.

7

Shame

The delivery room is a sacred place to me. I had the privilege of assisting in the deliveries of more than fifty babies as a medical student (and three more as an orthopedic surgeon!), and I was present at the births of all six of my children and one of my granddaughters. I've seen some pretty amazing things in my life, but nothing compares to childbirth.

On cue, the star of the show suddenly emerges from backstage amidst a flurry of activity and murmurs of delight from the small audience. *Wow!* He is gorgeous, a chip off the old divine block, love manifested in human form, indelibly stamped with the Maker's seal of approval. Regardless of the circumstances of his birth or the hard realities of his future, this will always be his true self, and to deeply *know* this about yourself is to experience joy. However, such life-giving self-awareness is very hard for parents to instill in their kids, and it rarely survives the gauntlet of childhood. For most people, the discovery of their true identity is a task for the second half of life.

According to Brené Brown, shame is the intensely painful feeling and belief that we are flawed and, therefore, unworthy of love and belonging. However, no one is born with shame, and there's not a whit of it in the newborn nursery. Shame is an acquired affliction. The doctrine of original innocence must surely have been written by a midwife.

I've identified three types of shame in my life—developmental, healthy, and situational—and they all feel the same: HEAVY. I'm reminded of the 1986 movie *The Mission*, in which Robert De Niro portrays a hot-blooded young man who kills his brother in a sword fight over a woman. Afterward, he is so filled with remorse that he gathers all of his brother's belongings, ties them up in a huge bundle, and drags it behind him everywhere he goes with a rope tied around his waist. In one iconic scene, he's struggling to climb a steep, muddy cliff in the Amazon during a rainstorm, the bundle repeatedly getting snagged and dragging him down, when a companion grabs a machete and hacks the rope in two. De Niro responds by silently retrieving the bundle, retying the rope, and continuing his exhausting climb. *Been there. Done that.*

Developmental shame (perhaps analogous to developmental trauma disorder) sneaks in on the heels of childhood trauma, quietly slips behind the curtain, and starts running the show. I grew up with the painful belief that I deserved my father's irritability and lack of interest because I wasn't a good enough kid. I thought there must be something fundamentally wrong with me, something irritating that made me unworthy of his love and affection. However, I'm sure that this was not my father's intent and that he was unaware of what was happening inside my young mind, which is what makes shame so pernicious and blame so misplaced.

Developmental shame's earliest evidence in my life was the emergence of the harsh voice of my inner critic. From as early as I can remember, I've said awful things to myself that I would never think about saying to anyone else. I saw a therapist for this and read books on self-compassion without much benefit. Nowadays, I regard the presence of relentless self-criticism in others as evidence of developmental shame.

By the end of childhood, we have our fixed window on reality and are left with either a clear lens of self-love or a dingy and distorted lens of shame—a "cataract of the soul." Mine was the latter. Bit by bit, shame was etched into the circuitry of my young brain. I wasn't too sure about self-love, either. I knew plenty of people who had too much of it, and I certainly didn't deserve it.

Father-wounding is a major producer of developmental shame in children, but it's not the only one. Being bullied, made fun of, or treated as insignificant by peers or coaches is devastating to a child's self-image, as is feeling different from others or not being able to live up to personal, religious, or moral standards. It's truly a wonder that anyone grows up feeling good about themselves.

When I was in junior high school, our low-tech precursor of social media was the "opinion book," a spiral notebook with a different student's name written at the top of every page. The idea was to secretly pass the notebook around the room during class time, flip through the pages, and write comments about each student on their page. Nasty comments were common since they were anonymous. I remember the anxiety that I felt one day when I saw an opinion book working its way toward me, knowing that my name was on one of those pages, and the relief that I felt when I saw that no one had dissed me. DKH (don't know him/her) was wonderfully neutral to read. I can't imagine the shame that today's kids must experience at the hands of their peers in this digital age.

Most dads try hard to provide for the needs of their children and to let them know that they are loved, although not always with words. With the best of intentions, they also try to mold their sons into their idea of "successful" men, typically utilizing more sticks than carrots. Failure to live up to a father's hopes, expectations, and demands is a major source of developmental shame for boys, and no mother can give her son what he needs from his dad.

The one thing that's missing in every case of father-wounding is this conveyed message from father to child: "You are precisely the person I love, enjoy, and want to be with, exactly as you are, and there is nothing you need to do—or ever can do—to earn or diminish my love for you."

I know from personal experience that healing from childhood trauma can be a tall order and a long process. How much better to prevent father-wounding in the first place! I'm convinced that if fathers everywhere conveyed this one missing message to their boys—in word, deed, and especially attuned energy—it would literally transform the world, one unconditionally loved son at a time. This should become the core teaching for fathers in new-parent classes. The outcomes of all other child-rearing philosophies would pale in comparison.

Guilt is about behavior: *I did something bad.* Whereas, shame is about identity: *I am bad.* Guilt and shame often overlap, and this isn't always a bad thing. In addition to my lifelong bundle of developmental shame, I dragged around a second bundle of healthy shame for being the sort of man who could have an affair and do what I had done. I deserved that second bundle and dragged it around for many years. But not forever. Healthy shame drove me to change, and there came a day when I could honestly say that I'm not the man I used to be.

Shame prevents the possibility of self-forgiveness, but at that point I was able to shift from shame to guilt, which gave me something priceless: a way to cut the rope. I couldn't change the past, but I found redemption by being honest and open, repenting, sincerely apologizing, asking for forgiveness, changing my behavior, and trying my best to make amends and heal relationships. (I identify with Jean Valjean and always get teary-eyed when I watch *Les Misérables*.)

For men, situational shame is failure—at work, with our children, in bed, in marriage, with money, with sports, with anything. It's being criticized, rejected, or made fun of. It's looking weak. It's knowing that we're not doing what we should in the eyes of someone important or that we're letting the team down. It's being incompetent, dismissed, ignored, or looked down upon. It's being used as a shining example of how not to do something.

Shame is so powerful because it's intensely personal, and we believe that we deserve it. We suffer through it alone, and there seems to be no way to change our defective core identity. We believe that if people knew who we really are, they would have nothing to do with us. Shame can be dangerous to experience and dangerous for others to be around. It often leads to depression, violence, and suicide. Addictions are common and are likely to be the result of shame rather than its cause.

Men have two basic modes of responding to shame: shut down (like me) or pissed off. I get flooded with emotion and can't think straight. My executive function goes offline, and my lizard brain takes over. I can't talk coherently, my stomach churns, and I avoid eye contact. My heart races, and my mouth feels dry. I feel like crying and want to run far away as quickly as possible. At the other extreme, many men who think they have rage issues are actually experiencing chronic shame.

No one is completely impervious to situational shame, but there are ways to become more shame-resistant. Learn to recognize when you're experiencing it in your body. I can feel myself starting to shut down physiologically, as described above. When you recognize the presence of shame, don't try to ignore or banish it. Instead, call it out by name to someone who has earned the right to hear you because the best way to quickly disarm shame is to own and expose it. "Hey, I'm experiencing shame right now, and here's what's going on . . ." Know your shame triggers. My biggies: *I'm a shitty dad and an incompetent geezer*. Reality check the messages and expectations that fuel shame and are whispering in your ear. *I'm not good enough or smart enough*. Is this really true? Finally, figure out what needs to happen right now to keep you from going off the rails, and act on it. *I need to be alone for about twenty minutes.*

REORDER

8

Graces

The great attraction of Christianity for folks like me (who've screwed the pooch) is the invitation to lay our sins at the foot of the cross and start over with a clean slate, whiter than snow. However, my previous religious experiences had mostly sucked. Then, Lori returned from a visit with her sister and told me that she had answered an "altar call" at church—*You did what?!*—and started attending a women's bible study. I noticed positive changes in her, which gave me the incentive to *again* try to get my own spiritual shit together.

After a few Sunday mornings of pulling into the parking lot, turning around, and driving back home again, I mustered the courage to reach out to a church leader I respected, who became a mentor for me. Under his tutelage, I joined a men's bible study, duly gave my life to Christ, and received divine forgiveness for my sins—to which my inner critic dryly remarked, *How nice for you*

. . . and convenient! I also volunteered to teach a couple of Sunday school classes, including (no joke) one called Experiencing God. Much later, I became a deacon at the church, and Lori and I joined a marriage enrichment team that put on weekend retreats similar to Marriage Encounter. I became a part of something bigger than myself and found what I most needed at the time: community.

Cutting to the chase, a long and deep run with Evangelicalism did not float my spiritual boat any more than Pentecostalism and Catholicism had done. My enthusiasm for an all-inclusive practice of Christianity did not mesh with the Evangelical worldview, and I became extremely judgmental of the judgmentalism that I witnessed in many of my fellow churchgoing sinners.

My strong bias is that our species is not neatly divided into saints and sinners. Rather, the line that separates good from evil runs right through the middle of every human heart, which means that we are all capable of anything, especially in the wake of trauma. I was also put off by so many certainties about who's saved and who's not.

Far off the beaten path by now, I kept my big toe in the church's belief system for years to maintain my community connections, but the massive white Evangelical support for our forty-fifth president eventually made it impossible for me to maintain that delicate balance. In the end, my quest for authenticity trumped my desire for mainstream belonging. Yogi Berra once said, "When you come to a fork in the road, take it," and that's what I did. Christianity and I had come a long way together. We wished each other well and went our separate ways.

The word *grace* used to piss me off. Why did Christians need to use this churchy word when there are so many others in common usage that fit the bill? Then I became the recipient of a ton of it, and I understood.

The expression "Wounded people wound people" doesn't begin to cover the reality of what Patti and our kids went through as a result of my actions. I understand the impact of childhood trauma in my life, but I don't blame father-wounding or claim victimhood for the decisions that I made. I always had agency, and when life was hard, I chose my own happiness over that of my wife and children. Furthermore, there is an element of luxury to my story: I moved to a different city, started a new life, built my career as a surgeon, got involved at church, had my sins forgiven, started a men's group, and years later wrote a memoir about my transformed life.

Meanwhile, Patti sat in the trenches with our kids. If you want a working definition of grace, find an example of "freely given, unmerited favor and love" in a wronged former spouse. Anger and unforgiveness are normal and totally justified responses to the trauma of infidelity. Perhaps the only thing more unfair is forgiveness.

When I moved out, Patti's large group of female friends rallied around her, and as time went by, she noticed that these women consisted of two main groups: There were those who focused on Patti's pain and her practical needs, and there were others whose main focus was their own pain that my cheating had triggered. The women in the latter group couldn't help feeding their anger to Patti, and eventually she realized this and quit meeting with them.

Patti started leading divorce recovery workshops at her parish and eventually got her master's degree and worked as a family therapist. One of our kids sent me an article she wrote for her local Catholic newspaper on forgiveness, and a big idea that stood out to me in this article was that unforgiveness is a poison that you drink every day in hopes that it will kill the person who hurt you. Forgiveness is a gift you give yourself because when you forgive someone, you set a prisoner free and then discover that the prisoner was you all along.

In time, Patti forgave me for everything, and I still don't know how she did it. She also walked the journey of reconciliation with me, which is not always possible or wise after forgiving someone. She treated me with kindness and respect at a time when I deserved only condemnation. At first, this heaped burning coals on my head and only added to my self-loathing. However, Patti's grace to me during the shitstorm of divorce was my first whiff of the aroma of heaven, and it cracked open a door deep inside me that had been bolted shut for as long as I could remember. Patti also modeled grace and forgiveness for our children, which has borne much fruit in their lives. Some of our kids have been through their own divorces and have followed their mom's example of kindness and respect with former spouses.

There are men and women in the Colorado Springs area who stepped into the void left by my absence, served as surrogate parents for my children, and pitched in to help Patti in ways that I will never know about. One of my sons was a math prodigy, two of them were talented hockey players, and my daughter was recognized as a "child of promise" at her elementary school. For the most part, I celebrated these and other amazing accomplishments from afar. I am deeply grateful for the village of saints who volunteered to stand in the gap for our kids in these areas and so many more.

Over a period of many years, I gradually learned to live with the paradox of becoming grateful for the consequences of things that I sincerely wish I'd never done. My story is not a script that I would ever recommend. Still, I eventually came to experience and witness in others the grace of having wounds transformed into gifts and of seeing good come out of evil.

As an example, sponsors are always recovering addicts in Alcoholics Anonymous because the core function of a sponsor is to share their experiences with those newly in recovery, offering guidance and support based on their own struggles and successes. I, too, was "gifted" in this way. Friends and family members started coming to me with requests to meet with men who were having affairs, and I was able to share with them the sobering realities of the path they were on, without judgment. Most of the time this was like talking to a brick wall, but dispelling a man's illusions occasionally helped to nudge him back on track.

Another example is that Lori and I have a daughter, son, and grandchildren whose very existence depended upon things happening as they did. I can't explain any of this—that's why they're called mysteries—but I've learned to embrace this tension of opposites with gratitude.

The most important thing I did for my children during those

hard years of long-distance parenting was to keep showing up. That sounds like a small thing, but it is not. I understand why some parents leave and never return because with each visit I had to face the music and experience a small taste of the consequences of my actions—a reality that Patti had to live with by herself every day. As much as I looked forward to being with my children, I was an emotional wreck for days before and after each visit.

For my own sanity, I sometimes convinced myself that my kids were okay, but they were not. They felt the shame of thinking they drove me away because they were bad kids. They got into trouble on purpose, thinking that it might bring me back. They projected their anger onto their mother and punched holes in the wall. Whenever we got together for a family meeting during my visits, I always tried to support Patti on disciplinary issues, to which my kids would say, in so many words, "Who the hell are you to be telling me what to do? You don't even live here!" I could only acknowledge that they were right, affirm that we were all doing our best under the circumstances, and keep coming back.

All four of my older children have forgiven me, each in their own way and their own timing, and I've never taken that for granted. I know divorced men who've repeatedly reached out to their estranged children but remain unforgiven. I've also learned that healing has a soft endpoint and that I need to be willing to revisit old wounds from time to time that have already been forgiven.

Lori, too, has extended a great deal of grace to me. She has loved me through many years of defensiveness, reactivity, and depression. She always fully supported my relationships with my older children, encouraged me to spend holidays with them, and welcomed them during visits and when they came to live with us. She has never kept score about how much time I've spent with them or complained about the financial realities of travel or supporting six children. I've always deeply appreciated how Patti and Lori have honored and supported each other in their parental roles, which is unique among the stories I've heard from other remarried men. I'm grateful that all six of my children treat each other as coequal siblings.

I decided one day to write down the conversations that always went through my head when I thought about my dad, and I came up with fourteen short, angry sentences, most of them laced with expletives. It made me bristle every time I read the list, and I shared it with a friend who volunteered to pray through the list with me, one item at a time. This took several months, but it softened me toward my father. I wanted to offer blanket forgiveness and be done with it, but every memory demanded its own act of forgiveness, some of them more than once. Forgiveness was both a process and a laundry list for me.

I eventually got healthy enough to talk to Dad about our relationship, but by then, the progression of his Alzheimer's disease made it impossible for him to understand what I was talking about. I remember standing in his backyard with Lori one day, crying my eyes out after a fruitless attempt to talk to Dad. As always with him, I was on my own.

Although forgiveness is essential for the healing of father-wounds, it doesn't always lead to reconciliation of relationships. Your dad may be deceased, unwilling, or unable to go there with you for a variety of reasons. There's probably a big discrepancy between how your dad thinks he raised you and your actual experiences of being raised by him, so keep this in mind if you choose to share your painful memories with him. He'll have a different interpretation of events than yours if he remembers them at all, and he might be inclined to set the record straight rather than listen to your story with empathy. I don't wish to discourage anyone who chooses the pathway of radical honesty with their father, but both of you will need to embrace the process with patience and humility for it to be fruitful.

In early November one year, when campgrounds were deserted but still open, I went camping with the intent of bringing to an end this long, drawn-out process of forgiving my dad. I fasted all day and spent time alone in the woods, as I had done as a boy. I brought pictures of my father and of myself, in addition to photos that represented my wounded child and inner protector. I sat by the fire all night and poured my heart out, tearfully speaking aloud the things I needed to say to Dad, and when I sensed that my work was done with each symbol, I placed it in the fire. After this overnight ritual, my anger was gone, and I felt only compassion for my father.

Dad eventually remarried, and after his second wife died, he lived alone for a couple of years, during which time his mental decline rapidly progressed. He moved in with my brother and his wife in Virginia for a few years and then moved to Tampa with my younger sister and her husband, who cared for him with remarkable kindness and good humor during his last years.

At ninety-four, Dad fell at home and hit his head. All five of us siblings gathered at the hospital, and after a few days it became clear that he wasn't going to survive. Semi comatose, he was scheduled to be discharged to a nursing home the next day, when I found myself alone with him for a few minutes. I lay down next to him in bed, held his hand, and told him how much I loved him, what a great dad he was, and how very proud I was to be his son. Then I kissed him, something I hadn't done since I was a boy, and he squeezed my hand. That afternoon, I flew back to Madison. This good man, my father, died two days later.

9

Rites

In my late fifties, a friend gave me a cassette tape of a talk by Richard Rohr on "The Journey of Spiritual Transformation" that blew me away. How did this Catholic priest, who had never met me or been married, know so much about my life? I looked up an article he had written for *Sojourners* magazine, titled "Boys to Men," that explained why males need rites of initiation, and I showed it to Lori, who pointed out a footnote that I had missed: Rohr's organization, the Center for Action and Contemplation, offered five-day retreats for men at various sites around the country, called the Men's Rites of Passage, or MROP. I found out where the next one was being held, sent in my application, and found myself on an airplane bound for Bend, Oregon, in May 2005. I didn't know a soul there. I only knew that this was where mine needed to be. The MROP was a major milestone that introduced me to a community of men who modeled healthy masculinity. Afterward, I did a deep dive into Rohr's teachings.

In 2008, I signed up for a backpacking trip to the Grand Canyon with a group of men from our church. The man organizing this venture knew of my enthusiasm for Rohr and was a fan, so he asked if I would speak to the men before we started our descent into the canyon the next morning. I illustrated some of what I had learned from Rohr with stories from my life, and this resonated with the men, who shared bits of their own stories with each other during the week. The Grand Canyon trip checked all the boxes for a once-in-a-lifetime male adventure. When we got back to Madison, there was a lot of interest in continuing to meet as a group, so I asked a friend to be my coleader, and we started meeting as a book club on Saturday mornings at church.

The format has evolved, men have come and gone, and there have been bumps in the road, but sixteen years later, our core group of about twenty men is still meeting regularly. Many of us also have close friendships with each other outside of our meetings. Basically, we get together and tell stories from our lives related to issues of interest to men. We don't judge each other for our struggles and failures, we're not a therapy or accountability group, and there's no preaching, fixing, or advice-giving. We try to speak and listen from the heart and agree to a code of confidentiality. That's it. No one is pressured to speak, but everyone is invited to do so. If you've ever been to a twelve-step meeting, this probably sounds familiar.

It's hard for me to convey the importance of these men in my life, but a good place to start is with a story. In 2019, Kelli Harding published the book *The Rabbit Effect: Live Longer, Happier, and Healthier with the Groundbreaking Science of Kindness*, which was inspired by a fascinating experimental study of the effect of a high-fat diet on rabbits. As expected, multiple cohorts of rabbits fed high-fat diets showed large fat deposits in their coronary arteries at autopsy. However, one group showed 60 percent fewer fatty deposits than all the others, and there was no obvious explanation for this. All of the rabbits were fed the same diets, were of the same genetic strain, and got the same amount of exercise.

When the investigators looked into it, they discovered that only one factor could explain the difference: the kindness shown to the healthier rabbits by the woman who cared for them. She talked softly to her bunnies while she cleaned their cages and tenderly cuddled them, like a doting pet owner. This remarkable study showed that love given to rabbits is literally good for their hearts. For Dr. Harding, it was just the beginning of a much larger story about the enormous impact of love, friendship, kindness, and life's purpose on our health and longevity.

I'm still in a leadership role in our men's group, but as the years have gone by, it has become obvious to me that I've been a bunny all along. No matter how we spend our time together, the hidden reality is that I have been experiencing intimacy with these men and microdosing on love for years—heck, occasionally even macrodosing. I'll bet my coronary arteries are 60 percent cleaner than they were in my fifties, thanks to these heart specialists that I call friends. They are agents of healing and transformation in my life.

They are also my vulnerability fitness group and safety net. I get to practice a whole range of uncertainty, risk, and emotional exposure with other men in a safe and confidential environment, which has gradually pumped up my capacity for marital intimacy and also eliminated the temptation to turn to other women to quench my thirst.

(Note: Illuman was created in 2012 as an organization to carry on the Men's Rites of Passage and as a spiritual movement to promote healthy masculinity and help men deepen our connections with ourselves, other men, and the needs of the world. All men are welcome, and virtual meetings are available. See Getting Started: Author's Suggested Resources.)

10

Therapy

Top-down and Bottom-up Modalities

The impact of trauma is stored in the body as well as the mind, and optimum therapy should address both. The top-down approach utilizes psychotherapy, social engagement, neurofeedback, and the processing of memories. In contrast, the bottom-up approach employs body-based activities such as yoga and breathwork as well as group activities like dancing, drumming, singing, and theater.

My personal experience with top-down therapy has included psychotherapy and EMDR (see below). Social engagement with my community of male friends has been my salvation, and almost nothing has been more therapeutic than meeting with my best friend for breakfast every week for the past decade. My study is lined with books geared toward self-help and spirituality.

My current bottom-up activities include pickleball, hiking, and drumming with other men at community gatherings. Years ago, I took a mindfulness-based stress-reduction (MBSR) class, which combines yoga and meditation, and I found it to be very helpful in managing my emotions around the time of my retirement.

Psychotherapy

No one goes to therapy because of their problems. We go to therapy because of our solutions. We seek therapy because solutions like alcohol, depression, perfectionism, anxiety, overeating, workaholism, or rage that helped us deal with a problem in the past have become overriding problems themselves.

In my late thirties, I started seeing a therapist in Colorado Springs for the consequences of infidelity, which was my solution to loneliness. I unfairly blamed that loneliness on my wife, but it was actually a consequence of my lifelong extreme independence, self-sufficiency, secrecy, and risk avoidance. At the time, I had no idea that father-wounding was the dormant volcano beneath a deep layer of developmental shame, distorted maps of reality that taught me what to expect from life, and a childhood survival strategy gone bad. It would take years and a great deal of perseverance to bore down through all of these layers to unhealed childhood trauma, which was my real problem.

I remember feeling confused and rather defensive when my therapist started asking questions about my relationship with my dad, seemingly within the first minute of our first meeting. Soon, however, he convinced me that there might be a tiny connection between my father issues and my recent behavior, so I continued working with him until I moved to Salt Lake City eight months later. I thought it shouldn't take more than three or four visits to wrap things up. All I needed to do was deconstruct my story in order to see the big picture and move on.

Contrary to my expectation, however, my therapist validated my feelings but not my story! He pointed out contradictions and gently called me out whenever I shifted from telling my story to telling other people's stories. He knew that my story was the creation of my own mind and neither objective nor accurate. I'm grateful for his wisdom. If he had validated my story, I'd probably still be seeing him and stuck in the same old narrative.

What struck me right away was the fact that I had so few detailed memories from childhood, most notably my toothache story, and the rest consisted of little snippets of sensory flashbacks and general interpretations of my father's moods and behavior. I had very limited recall of details from my past but impeccable emotional memory, which is typical of all trauma stories.

My therapist reminded me of Police Sergeant Joe Friday when he was interviewing a crime scene witness in the old TV series, *Dragnet*: "Just the facts, ma'am." This boiled down to what my father actually said and didn't say and to what he actually did and didn't do. For example, I don't really know that Dad thought of me as a nuisance, that my needs and desires weren't important to him, or that he didn't enjoy my company. These were my interpretations of his behavior, and they might or might not be accurate. This is an important distinction because it helped me see my father as a complex soul with his own story rather than just a caricature in mine. It also helped me loosen my grip on my identity as a victim, which otherwise might have imprisoned me in my own narrative.

Looking back, I see the progression of my healing journey reflected in my evolving attitude about my story. I began with unwavering curiosity and determination to fearlessly explore my relationship with my father, which brought to light an ocean of repressed anger and rivers of sadness. With time, I developed compassion for Dad, owned the story as my own creation, and no longer blamed anyone, including myself. In the end, the gift of therapy was a new point of view that put my childhood story in its proper perspective. It was no longer the defining story of my life, and I was able to hold it lightly and with gratitude.

I'm grateful to my therapist for helping me acknowledge my trauma, identify my wounds, and find a measure of self-compassion as first steps on my healing journey. However, when I left for Utah, I was still decades away from any transformational change.

EMDR

Eye Movement Desensitization and Reprocessing, or EMDR, had its beginning as a chance observation. In 1987, psychologist Francine Shapiro was walking through a park when she noticed a consistent pattern: When she was thinking about painful memories, her eyes spontaneously moved back and forth, and this produced great relief from the disturbing thoughts. Intrigued, Shapiro subjected her observations to years of research and gradually developed EMDR into a treatment protocol that has proven to be effective in the treatment of trauma.

This sounds a bit woo-woo, but I've been open to unusual treatment options since my arthritis experiences many years ago, so after learning about EMDR in Bessel van der Kolk's book, *The Body Keeps the Score*, I did a Google search and found a therapist in my area who specialized in trauma, was trained in the protocol, and accepted my health insurance coverage. I saw her every other week for about nine months, and we started doing EMDR on my second or third visit. Rather than eye movement, I held a small rubber pad in each hand during our sessions, through which she caused a vibration to switch back and forth from left to right at variable intervals and intensities.

My therapist asked me to think about a traumatic memory of my choosing with my eyes closed and then watched for signs of emotional activation. I didn't need to tell her what I was thinking about, but she was open to conversation whenever I wanted to talk. When I showed signs of emotional arousal, she encouraged me to "Notice that" and asked what I was feeling in my body. Periodically, I was instructed to "Stay with that" and to slowly take a few deep breaths. She also asked, "What's next?" from time to time. During these EMDR sessions, long-forgotten snippets of memories filled my thoughts, one leading to the next, willy-nilly, many of them seemingly unrelated to the disturbing memory with which I'd started. These sessions were often followed by nights of vivid dreams.

Here's what was truly amazing: After only the second EMDR session, I began to notice a substantial reduction in my reactivity to Lori's way of talking to me. One day, we were driving to Chicago when she said something that hurt me, and with great difficulty, I told her how I was feeling and why. She was genuinely surprised by my reaction, and after we talked about it, Lori apologized. This was the first time in my life that I was able to talk about what I was experiencing in the midst of a flashback.

After languishing in my default mode of silently avoiding conflict for so many years, I was astonished by how rapidly I got better at this. That's not to say it was easy—far from it—but during those nine months of treatment, I learned how to argue with Lori, push back, and stand up for myself. Finally, I was able to give her immediate feedback on how I experienced her words, tone of voice, and body language.

EMDR was transformational for me personally and also for our marriage. It enabled me to engage in conflict and be real with Lori for the first time, and it also gave her the opportunity to make changes of her own. I don't know how things would have turned out if she had dug in her heels when I was learning to establish communication boundaries, but her willingness to change along with me was an act of love that deeply touched me. Lori is much kinder and more empathetic than she once was. She has honed these skills as a married woman, much to her credit.

No one really knows how EMDR works, but there's a correlation with how we process memories during REM (rapid eye movement) sleep. In some mysterious way, EMDR reprocessed and integrated traumatic memories into the overall narrative of my life, which restored my sense of agency and ownership of my thoughts and behavior. At seventy, this was my first experience of transformational change in the treatment of father-wounding.

11
MDMA

You will come, at a turning of the trail,
to a wall of flame.

After the hard climb and the exhausted dreaming,
you will come to a place where
he with whom you have walked this far will stop,

will stand beside you on the treacherous, steep path
and stare as you shiver at the moving wall, the flame
that blocks your vision of what comes after.

And that one, who you thought would accompany you
always,
who held your face tenderly a little while in his hands—
who pressed the palms of his hands into drenched grass
and washed from your cheeks the soot, the tear-tracks—

he is telling you now
that all that stands between you
and everything you have known since the beginning

is this: this wall.

Between yourself and the beloved,
between yourself and your joy,
the riverbank swaying with wildflowers,

the shaft of sunlight on the rock, the song.
Will you pass through it now?

Will you let it consume whatever solidness this is
you call your life, and send you out, a tremor of heat,
a radiance, a changed flickering thing?

—"Questo Muro" (This Wall) by Anita Barrows

I had done my homework. I sat on the sofa and looked over the symbols and pictures that I had arranged, just so, on the coffee table. The candle was lit, the fireplace aglow, and meditation music softly played in the background. I reviewed my intention for this, my first MDMA trip: *I want to love like I've never been hurt before.* I lay down, smiled at Lori, and closed my eyes as the medicine took effect.

There are no adequate words for a transcendent experience, but here's what comes to mind when I think about that day: I passed through that wall of flame, and a ton of debris in my life was incinerated in the passage. The lifelong voice of my inner critic disappeared and has never returned. My armor melted away like wax, and my cataract of the soul was replaced with a clear lens of self-love. I met the Beloved, the One whom I had been seeking all my life, and for the first time, I fully experienced how deeply I am loved, have always been loved, and will always be loved. *Such joy, peace, and gratitude!* Within those precious few hours I stepped into a new reality, and this unitive mystical experience changed my life. When I opened my eyes, I recognized the beautiful smile of the Beloved on the face of my wife and found myself clothed in my true identity as a deeply loved son, father, and husband. Other than that, it was a pretty ordinary day.

After the trip, I journaled and talked about my experience with Lori and a few close friends and family members—all part of post-trip integration, which is so important when working with trauma. Through the integration process, I realized that there was more work to be done on my healing journey, so I took additional MDMA trips about every four months over two years, each with specific intentions. "Set and setting," shorthand for mindset (intentions) and physical environment, are critically important factors that determine the type of experience and outcome of psychedelic trips in the treatment of trauma.

I felt the need to revisit my toothache story and did this on two occasions. The first time, I experienced an idealized response from my parents, who comforted me and then drove me to a specialist in children's dentistry who painlessly took care of my problem. Afterward, Mom and Dad listened and asked questions as I told them what the experience was like for me.

The second time, Mom wasn't there, and I reversed roles with Dad. He was crying, and I held him in my scrawny ten-year-old arms and rubbed his back while whispering, "Oh, Honey," as he told me how hard it was for him when his dad died, how devastating it was when Mom left him for another man, and the deep shame he felt for not being able to provide financially for his family. When he finished crying, I gently wiped away his tears and assured him that he was going to be okay, I was going to be okay, and we were going to be okay, but right now he needed to take me to a dentist.

Quiet and hidden for nearly three-quarters of a century, developmental shame was the hardest nut to crack and the last barrier to fall on my healing journey. In the end, during a trip, I was given the gift of seeing myself through the eyes and heart of my wife. I experienced Lori's great love for me as never before, and the myth of being a burden vanished from my life.

I discovered that my soul can't tell the difference between an MDMA trip and reality. I'd always understood that the past is unalterable, and the best we can hope for is to write the ending of our story. However, this drug has been shown experimentally to temporarily open a child-like period of brain plasticity. With each trip, I was able to rewrite a chapter from my early life.

Healing wasn't about gaining a new understanding of what happened; it was about safely going back and changing the story. These new positive memories now coexist with old trauma memories and have superseded them in importance. In psychological parlance, I experienced a chemically aided reactivation and disconfirmation of problematic childhood beliefs, or schema. But in practical terms, my very realistic experience with MDMA was that of time travel. I'm living proof that it's never too late to have a happy childhood.

Finally, after these additional experiences, I knew that my work was done. After breaking the logjam, the river started to flow, and my joy and gratitude never diminished after I stopped taking the drug. As time went by, it became clear that this was a new season of life for me, not just a passing phenomenon. I had reached the summit of healing from childhood trauma as a seventy-five-year-old, which probably makes me a contender for a spot in the *Guinness World Records*.

When I think of all of the milestone events, loved ones, teachers, seeking, suffering, grace, forgiveness, inner work, community, and deep friendships that have gone into my crockpot during these many years, slowly cooking me into a savory stew, I know that MDMA is not a miracle drug. It was just the right catalyst that came along at the right time in my life, and for that, I am grateful beyond words.

After trauma, it's almost impossible to think your way into a new way of living. Deeply felt experiences are the stuff of transformation. However, psychedelics are obviously not the only way to rewire your emotional brain circuitry. The key is to be temporarily taken out from behind the steering wheel of normal life. Hitting bottom, great suffering, and great love come to mind, as does experiencing the birth of a child, faithful adherence to a contemplative practice like meditation or yoga, or having a profound spiritual experience. Healing can happen in a moment while merely standing in the laundry detergent aisle at Piggly Wiggly.

Inner healing was also associated with physical healing for

me. After thirty years of seasonal misery, I've had no paper cuts in my hands for the past two winters despite using no medications or superglue. I hesitate to say that I'm cured of psoriasis because this could all come back tomorrow, but my digital bunnies have given me impressive confirmation that I'm really and truly, finally okay. I can't wait to see how my prostate responds.

Although I came of age during the sixties, I had no interest in psychedelics until I started learning about trauma as a senior citizen. MDMA was touted as a highly successful drug for PTSD in many local and national news reports, and I discovered that Madison is a hotbed of research on the therapeutic effects of psychedelics. I dove into the research and applied to be part of a Phase 3 clinical trial of MDMA-assisted psychotherapy for PTSD. However, I wasn't accepted into the study, probably because I didn't meet the strict diagnostic criteria for PTSD. As mentioned earlier, this is true of most childhood trauma survivors.

Also known as ecstasy or molly, MDMA is currently designated as a Schedule I drug under the US Controlled Substances Act, which means that it is strictly prohibited and illegal to possess. It also has risks and potential problems beyond the medical and legal ones. For one, life is hard, and this drug can become just another way to numb and avoid pain. In addition, MDMA seems to offer the possibility of emotional exposure without those pesky sidekicks of uncertainty and risk—in other words, intimacy without vulnerability. Indeed, there is a role for this in MDMA-assisted couples therapy, which can enable partners to have difficult conversations in a safe environment.

Phase 3 clinical trials have shown remarkable long-term success with PTSD, but in August 2024, the FDA denied a new drug application that would have made MDMA the first psychedelic to be approved for medical use. The main sticking point was the impossibility of doing double-blind studies with a drug that exerts its beneficial effects by creating transcendent experiences. Anyone in such a study can easily tell whether they got the drug or a placebo. In fact, the more powerful the transcendent experience, the more therapeutic the effect, as was my experience.

However, transcendence can't be measured, which makes scientists uneasy, and there's no obvious solution to this problem because double-blind studies remain the gold standard of scientific inquiry. Drug companies are working to harness the therapeutic effects of psychedelics without the associated altered states of consciousness, but it appears likely that a transcendent experience is simply what it feels like to have a critical period of brain plasticity opened.

Another major concern with MDMA is that it's a manufactured drug that can only be obtained from illegal sources. You can't grow it in your basement. You have to procure it, which is risky business. There are commercially available test kits that can screen for the presence of fentanyl and other contaminants, but you can never be sure about what you're getting on the black market.

Another problem is that the current protocol for Phase 3 clinical trials requires the presence of two trained therapists, ideally a woman and a man, to be present for the duration of a client's psychedelic experience, which can last up to eight hours. This protocol also typically includes an overnight stay and is scheduled to happen once a month for three months, with talk therapy in between. This makes sense from a therapeutic and safety perspective, but who's going to pay for it? As often happens, those with financial means are most likely to have access to treatment, whereas those without means are most likely to need it.

Finally, client safety is a real concern with a prosocial drug like MDMA, which is not only a psychedelic but also an empathogen that generates intense feelings of trust and goodwill. This is ideal for PTSD treatment, but it also makes clients susceptible to abuse without strict safeguards.

I believe that MDMA-assisted psychotherapy for PTSD is unlikely to be legalized in the near future for several reasons. In addition to the double-blind problem, the mentality of the "war on drugs" that began during the Nixon era is still prevalent. Nancy Reagan's "Just Say No!" and the frying egg in "This Is Your Brain on Drugs" campaign had their intended effect on public opinion, which will likely undermine support for research on the therapeutic properties of psychedelics for years to come. In the meantime, being tough on crime is always a vote-getter.

We are on the cusp of an exciting breakthrough in the treatment of trauma and other mental health conditions with psychedelics, which can be powerful tools in the proper setting and with appropriate guardrails. I'm hopeful that MDMA-assisted psychotherapy will someday be legalized for PTSD, but small-t trauma, even with large-C consequences, will never make the cut.

12

Dear Dads

Dear Dads,

If you suspect that your son (or daughter) has a big father-wound and you want to do something about it, great work! You're already 80 percent there. If it's true, however, it probably won't be productive to come right out and ask if you've wounded him, guns blazing, because he knows very well when he's not safe.

For anything new to happen, you'll need to enter his world with a willingness to listen and learn. I can't tell you how to do this, but he can if you ask. Maybe that's a good place to start. If you find the path of healing, you won't be in control. This might be a new experience for you.

Ask what he wants and needs from you, and listen from your heart. Answer questions truthfully, but don't overwhelm him with too much information. He already knows a lot more about you and your story than you think he does. Focus on what's good for him, not on what will make you feel better. He's not a priest, and you're not there for confession.

Don't try to correct his misconceptions or faulty memories, and don't attempt to explain the reasons for things you've done or failed to do unless he asks. This is where you'll probably need to bite your tongue until it bleeds a little. His experience is far more important than your version of events, and he can already lip-sync your justification song.

Apologize and ask for forgiveness if you can do it honestly. He might need to hear this more than once, and he'll know if you're just mouthing the words. Respect his beliefs and traditions, and don't try to squeeze him into yours. Model the grace and forgiveness that you wish to receive.

Suggest getting away for a day or two, doing whatever he thinks might be healing. Plan this together and make it your top priority. Pick a place with privacy where you can respectfully express emotion and be emotional. Agree to a pact of confidentiality to make this a safe space, and don't share anything with anyone afterward without his permission.

Father-wounding doesn't account for all of the pain in his life, so don't beat yourself up with that misconception, and don't make every conversation a heavy experience. Talk about positive memories, too, and do stuff that's fun. Laugh together whenever you can. Few things are more healing in a relationship.

Talk about how each of you would like things to be different from now on, but don't expect too much from your efforts. The hope for change can quickly become the expectation of change, which sets you up for disappointment and anger. Chip away at healing your relationship, and be content with little victories. Keep showing up. Keep trying. I'm really proud of you!

Hugs, Keith

13

Return to Joy

The sign
that it's finally
healed

is when a wound
is alchemized
into a story

that dresses
the wound
of another.

—"It's Finally Healed" by Chelan Harkin

I don't know very many fully adult humans, but I know a lot of middle-aged and elderly children who are limping around the playground and trying their best to act like grown-ups. I recognize them because it takes one to know one. Father-wounding does that to us. We grow up and grow old while remaining emotionally frozen in time as children who keep trying to save us from disasters. "If a nuclear bomb explodes, hide under your desk." "If there's a monster under your bed, keep the light on." "If you have a toothache, pretend you're okay." Adorable. I should post these on my refrigerator.

For years, I kept a picture on my desk of a sad little boy holding his hand to his cheek as though he had a toothache—an icon of my inner wounded child. I looked at that picture and talked to the boy in my mind every day, and he did something for me that took a long time to appreciate: He put a human face on father-wounding. He kept reminding me that healing isn't just about how to recover from something that happened in the past. It's also about what to do now with that little boy who still lives inside me.

This is self-love: You need that little kid who wants to save you more than you realize. He's very much alive, and you need him to come out of hiding and grow up under your guidance to experience wholeness. Although you've been carrying him around all these years, he doesn't know what you know and hasn't walked a mile in your shoes. He's inexperienced and naive, so you'll need to show him the ropes, and he'll need to show you some of the good stuff you've forgotten.

Keep a picture of yourself at a young age on your phone and look at it often. He'll like that. Develop a relationship with him in your imagination, and make it as tangible as possible with pictures and meaningful symbols. Only love can heal the wounded child within you, and loving that child doesn't require special training or precautions because no one overdoses on kindness. You can't get it wrong. Your intention and effort are all that matter.

I sometimes feel like that kid in the movie *The Sixth Sense*: I see wounded people everywhere, and that recognition is just an example of the gifts that young Keith brings me. I get to parent him now in ways that my father couldn't, and honestly, sometimes I hope he never grows up. I'm having wonderful dreams in which we're going places and doing things together, and I've stopped trying to rescue him. Now I just smile when I see him and give him my undivided attention. That's all he ever really wanted anyway.

I learned the hard way that no one finds the sort of happiness we're all looking for by chasing after it. Happiness is a wonderful feeling, but it's short-lived and fragile. On many occasions, I've literally been happy one minute and unhappy the next when one of my sensitivities has been triggered, or things haven't gone my way. I think of happiness as life's consolation prize for being so difficult. It doesn't store well, so we need to be constantly foraging for more of it, and that's the tipoff to the true nature of happiness. How much is enough? *More. Always more.* The pursuit of happiness, our American dream, turns out to be just another addiction.

Everyone wants to be happy, of course, and I'm no exception, but I've learned to hold happiness lightly when it comes my way. I have a strong tendency to turn a good thing into the ultimate thing, and every time I do this, it moves in and takes over the house. I'm either happy that I have my heart's desire, sad and angry that I don't, or worried that I'm about to lose it. The "shoulds," "shouldn'ts," and "if onlys" of life still promise to fulfill my longings, but I've learned from years of experience that they never deliver the goods.

In fact, we think we long for happiness, but that isn't really true. We actually long for joy but settle for happiness. Joy is the opposite of loneliness, and it's also much more than a feeling. For me, it's a Presence, a lightness, an equanimity that abides through the ups and downs of life. It's deeply knowing my true identity. It's enjoying people who used to annoy me. It's a handwritten invitation to the Big Dance.

Years ago, I began to catch glimpses of joy out of the corner of my eye when I started showing up every day with a willingness to live the life I've been given on its own terms, no longer on terms dictated by what I want and think I deserve. This was so countercultural that it was hard going for a long time, but I can see now that I've always and only experienced joy right here, right now, with what is—full stop. Nevertheless, inner work and self-improvement projects aren't wasted effort. In some mysterious way, our strivings broaden the bandwidth of our capacity to receive love, and what is joy other than diminished resistance to the boundless love within which we already live and move and have our being?

I often talk about this season of joy and gratitude, but it doesn't mean that I'm shielded from suffering. On the contrary, putting away my armor and having an open heart has enabled me to drink deeply from the well of joy and sorrow, which are not separate. Also, "loving like I've never been hurt before" hasn't meant loving and never being hurt again. It has created within me a willingness and newfound capacity to have my heart broken by the things that break the Beloved's heart.

Life will always be difficult in many ways, as it is for everyone, but I'm able to handle whatever comes my way now as a healthy man rather than a wounded child. This is a major shift from survival mode to sacred dance, from treading water to surfing. The freedom to know what I know and feel what I feel is the true gift of healing. There's nothing to hide, numb, or run away from anymore. *Rich* is the word that comes to mind when I think about this season of life, and I wouldn't trade it for anything.

More than anything, I wish the same for you, whatever your age. A good place to start is by developing vulnerable relationships with other men and working on forgiveness. Next steps might include watching the movie *The Wisdom of Trauma*, reading *The Body Keeps the Score*, finding a trauma therapist who offers EMDR, and joining a yoga class. Investigate other treatment options that make sense for you. (See Getting Started: Author's Suggested Resources.)

We are living in an unprecedented time in human history that's overflowing with unmet needs, large and small. Find your community and take your pick. This hurting world needs you, and the greatest gift you can give the world is your own transformation. You are not alone in this.

Getting Started

(Author's Suggested Resources)

Addiction

Maté, MD, Gabor. *In the Realm of Hungry Ghosts: Close Encounters with Addiction*. Vermillion, an imprint of Penguin Random House, 2010.

Rohr, Richard. *Breathing Under Water: Spirituality and the Twelve Steps*. Franciscan Media, 2021.

Forgiveness

Smedes, Lewis B. *The Art of Forgiving: When You Need to Forgive and Don't Know How*. Random House, 1996.

Yancey, Philip. *What's So Amazing About Grace?* Revised and Updated. Zondervan, 2023.

Health and Healing

Harding, MD, MPH, Kelli. *The Rabbit Effect: Live Longer, Happier, and Healthier with the Groundbreaking Science of Kindness*. Simon and Schuster, 2019.

MDMA

Nuwer, Rachel. *I Feel Love: MDMA and the Quest for Connection in a Fractured World*. Bloomsbury Publishing, 2023.

Men's Groups

Illuman (illuman.org)
ManKind Project (mkpusa.org)

Order-Disorder-Reorder

Rohr, Richard. *The Universal Christ: How a Forgotten Reality Can Change Everything We See, Hope For, and Believe*. Convergent Books, 2019.

Shame

Brown, Brené. *Men, Women, and Worthiness: The Experience of Shame and the Power of Being Enough*. Sounds True, Audible Audiobook, 2013.

Trauma

Maté, MD, Gabor, with Daniel Maté. *The Myth of Normal: Trauma, Illness, and Healing in a Toxic Culture*. Penguin Random House, 2022.

Rohr, Richard, with Joseph Martos. "Father Hunger" and "The Father Wound." In *From Wild Man to Wise Man: Reflections on Male Spirituality*. St. Anthony Messenger Press, 2005.

The Wisdom of Trauma. Directed by Maurizio Benazzo and Zaya Benazzo, featuring Gabor Maté, MD. 2021. https://www.thewisdomoftrauma.com.

van der Kolk, Bessel, MD. *The Body Keeps the Score: Brain, Mind, and Body in the Healing of Trauma*. Penguin Random House, 2014.

Acknowledgments

"Questo Muro" (This Wall), from *Kindred Flame: Six Poems* by Anita Barrows. Copyright 2008 by Anita Barrows. Used with permission of the poet.

"It's Finally Healed," from *Let Us Dance!: The Stumble and Whirl with the Beloved* by Chelan Harkin. Copyright 2021 by Chelan Harkin. Used with permission of the poet.

About the Author

Keith Kahle is a retired orthopedic surgeon and first-time author. He brings a seasoned, compassionate lens to the emotional and spiritual dimensions of healing from childhood trauma, drawing upon decades of professional experience, a tenacious quest for personal  wholeness, and a lifetime desire to bring healing to others. He and his wife live in Madison, Wisconsin.

Printed in the United States
by Baker & Taylor Publisher Services